— Great Themes of the Bible —

COVENANT:

God's Living Covenant

ABINGDON PRESS

NASHVILLE

GREAT THEMES OF THE BIBLE
Covenant: God's Living Covenant

Copyright © 2006 by Abingdon Press

ISBN 0-687-49130-4

This book is printed on recycled, acid-free, and elemental-chlorine–free paper.

MANUFACTURED IN THE UNITED STATES OF AMERICA

06 07 08 09 10 11 12 13 14 15—10 9 8 7 6 5 4 3 2 1

Table of Contents

Welcome to
Great Themes of the Bible

We are pleased that you have chosen *Great Themes of the Bible* for your small-group study. This series of study books cultivates faith formation in contemporary life using reliable principles of Christian education to explore major themes of the Bible, the issues and questions generated by these themes, and how the Bible illuminates our response to them in daily life. The sessions provide many opportunities for spiritual growth through worship, study, reflection, and interaction with other participants.

Great Themes of the Bible Cultivates Faith Formation in Contemporary Life

Who is God? How is God at work in our world? How does God call us and relate to us? How do we relate to God and to one another? What does Jesus Christ reveal to us about God? What is the potential for life in which we choose to be committed to God through Jesus Christ? How do we find hope? Such questions are at the heart of faith formation in contemporary life.

The Bible presents great themes that are universally relevant for the faith formation of all human beings in all times and places. Great themes such as call, creation, covenant, Christ, commitment, and community provide points of encounter between contemporary life and the times, places, and people in the Bible. As we reflect upon faith issues in our daily lives, we can engage biblical themes in order to learn more about God and in order to interpret what it means to live with faith in God.

The great themes of the Bible are the great themes of life. They generate questions and issues today just as they did for those in the biblical world. As we identify and explore these themes, we also engage the related questions and issues as they emerge in our contemporary life and culture. Exploring the Bible helps us see how people in the biblical world dealt with the issues and questions generated by a particular theme. Sometimes they responded exactly the way we would respond. Other times, they responded quite differently. In every case, however, we can glimpse God at work as we compare and contrast their situations with our own.

In Christian faith formation, we delve again and again into the Bible as we reflect upon our daily lives in light of Christian teaching. One way to imagine this process is by envisioning a spiral. A theme in the Bible generates questions and issues. We reflect upon the theme and consider the questions and issues it raises in our contemporary lives. We read the Bible and ask ourselves how the stories and teachings inform the theme and its questions and issues. We reflect upon the insights we have gained and perhaps make adjustments in our lives. We spiral through a particular theme and its issues and questions more than once as we look to the Bible for help, guidance, and hope. As we participate in this ongoing process, we gain deeper awareness of who God is and what God wants us to do, to be, and to become. The books in the *Great Themes of the Bible* series are structured around this spiraling process of faith formation.

Theme

Bible

Issues and Questions in Contemporary Life

Great Themes of the Bible Is Built Upon Reliable Christian Education Principles

The sessions in each of the books in *Great Themes Of The Bible* are based on the Scriptures and lesson guides in the *Uniform Series of International Bible Lessons for Christian Teaching.* These guides provide reliable Christian education principles to those who write the books. Session development for a book in *Great Themes of the Bible* is guided by a unifying principle that illuminates the unity between life and the Bible by emphasizing a key theme. The principle contains three components: a life statement, a life question, and a biblical response.

The lesson guides also include statements for every Scripture that help the writer to think about and develop the sessions. These statements occur in five categories or matrices: Learner, Scripture, Faith Interaction, Teaching Strategies, and Special Interest.

Statements in the Learner matrix identify general characteristics describing life stages, developmental issues, and particular experiences (special needs, concerns, or celebrations) that characterize learners.

Statements in the Scripture matrix identify a variety of key issues, questions, practices, and affirmations raised from the biblical texts. These may include historical, cultural, ethical, and theological perspectives.

Statements in the Faith Interaction matrix identify ways in which learners and Scripture might interact in the context of the Bible study. The statements relate to personal, communal, and societal expressions of faith.

Statements in the Teaching Strategies matrix suggest ways for writers to create sessions that connect Scripture and learners through a variety of educational methods that take into account the different ways people learn.

Statements in the Special Interest matrix identify ways writers might address topics of special concern that are particularly appropriate to the Scripture text: handicapping conditions, racial and ethnic issues, drug and alcohol abuse, and ecology, for example.

While the Faith Interaction matrix provides the beginning point for each session in a book in the *Great Themes of the Bible,* learning goals employed by the writers arise from all these matrices.

Great Themes of the Bible Provides Opportunities for Spiritual Growth

The books in *Great Themes of The Bible* offer you an opportunity to see the vital connection between daily life and the Bible. Every session begins and ends with worship in order to help you experience God's presence as you participate in the sessions. The small group sessions also provide opportunities to develop friendships with others that are based upon respect, trust, and mutual encouragement in faith formation.

WELCOME TO *GREAT THEMES OF THE BIBLE*

The following principles guide our approach to spiritual growth and faith formation:

- Faith and life belong together. We seek to discover connections or crossing points between what God reveals in the Bible and the needs, choices, and celebrations of our ordinary experience. Biblical themes provide this crossing point.
- Everyone is a theologian. *Theology* may be defined as "loving God with our minds" as well as with our hearts. All in your group, regardless of background, are fully qualified to do that.
- Adults learn best through reflection on experience. No longer are we blank tablets on which new knowledge must be imprinted. We can draw on a fund of experiences and ask what it means for us in light of Scripture and Christian teaching about God and creation.
- Questions stimulate spiritual growth more than answers. An authoritative answer seems final and discourages further thinking, while a stimulating question invites further creative exploration and dialogue.
- Learning involves change, choice, and pain. If we are to take seriously what God is telling us in Scripture, we must be open to changing our opinions, making new lifestyle choices, and experiencing the pain of letting go of the old and moving into a new and unknown future, following the God of continuing creation.
- Community sharing fosters spiritual growth. When a group commits to struggling together with questions of faith and life, they share personal experiences, challenge assumptions, deepen relationships, and pray. God's Spirit is present. The God of continuing creation is at work.

We pray that you will experience the freedom to ask questions as you explore the great themes in your life and in the Bible. We pray that you will encounter and experience the life-transforming love of God as you become part of a *Great Themes of the Bible* group. And finally, we pray that you will see yourself as a beloved human being created in the image of God and that you will grow in your love of God, self, and neighbor.

Using the Books in
Great Themes of the Bible

Each book in the *Great Themes of the Bible* series has within its pages all you need to lead or to participate in a group.

At the beginning of each book you will find:

- suggestions for organizing a *Great Themes of the Bible* small group.
- suggestions for different ways to use the book.
- suggestions for leading a group.
- an introduction to the great theme of the Bible that is at the center of all the sessions.

In each of the seven sessions you will find:

- a focus statement that illuminates the particular issues and questions of the theme in contemporary life and in the Scriptures for the session.
- opening and closing worship experiences related to the focus of each session.
- concise, easy-to-use leader/learner helps placed in boxes near the main text to which they refer.
- main content rich with illustrations from contemporary life and reliable information about the Scriptures in each session.

In the Appendix you will find:

- a list of Scriptures that illuminate the biblical theme.
- information about the Committee on the Uniform Series.

Books in the *Great Themes of the Bible* series are designed for versatility of use in a variety of settings.

Small Groups on Sunday Morning. Sunday morning groups usually meet for 45 minutes to an hour. If your group would like to go into greater depth, you can divide the sessions and do the study for longer than seven weeks.

Weekday or Weeknight Groups. We recommend 60 to 90 minutes for weekday/weeknight groups. Participants should prepare ahead by reading the content of the session and choosing one activity for deeper reflection and study. A group leader may wish to assign these activities.

A Weekend Retreat. For a weekend retreat, distribute books at least two weeks in advance. Locate and provide additional media resources and reference materials, such as hymnals, Bibles, Bible dictionaries and commentaries, and other books. If possible, have a computer with Internet capabilities on site. Tell participants to read their study books before the retreat. Begin on Friday with an evening meal or refreshments followed by gathering time and worship. Review the introduction to the theme. Do the activities in Session 1. Cover Sessions 2, 3, 4, 5, and 6 on Saturday. Develop a schedule that includes time for breaks, meals, and personal reflection of various topics and Scriptures in the sessions. Cover Session 7 on Sunday. End the retreat with closing worship on Sunday afternoon.

Individual Devotion and Reflection. While the books are designed for small-group study, they can also be beneficial for individual devotion and reflection. Use the book as a personal Bible study resource. Read the Scriptures, then read the main content of the sessions. Adapt the questions in the leader/learner boxes to help you reflect upon the issues related to the biblical theme. Learning with a small group of persons offers certain advantages over studying alone. In a small group, you will encounter people whose life experiences, education, opinions and ideas, personalities, skills, talents, and interests may be different from yours. Such differences can make the experience of Bible study richer and more challenging.

Organizing a *Great Themes of the Bible* Small Group

Great Themes of the Bible is an excellent resource for all people who are looking for meaning in their daily lives, who want to grow in their faith, and who want to read and reflect upon major themes in the Bible. They may be persons who are not part of a faith community yet who are seekers on a profound spiritual journey. They may be new Christians or new members who want to know more about Christian faith. Or they may be people who have been in church a long time but who feel a need for spiritual renewal. All such persons desire to engage more deeply with issues of faith and with the Bible in order to find meaning and hope.

Great Themes of the Bible is an excellent small-group study for those who are not yet involved in an ongoing Bible study, for those who prefer short-term rather than long-term studies, or for those who have never been involved in any kind of Bible study.

Starting a *Great Themes of the Bible* study group is an effective way to involve newcomers in the life of your local church. If you want to start a *Great Themes of the Bible* small group as part of the evangelism program in your local church, follow the steps below.

- Read through the *Great Themes of the Bible* study book. Think about the theme, the issues generated by the theme, and the Scriptures. Prepare to respond to questions that someone may ask about the study.

- Develop a list of potential participants. An ideal size for a small group is 7 to 12 people. Your list should have about twice your target number (14 to 24 people). Have your local church purchase a copy of the study book for each of the persons on your list.

- Decide on a location and time for your *Great Themes of the Bible* group. Of course, the details can be negotiated with those persons who accept the invitation; but you need to sound definitive and clear to prospective group members. "We will initially set Wednesday night from 7 to 9 P.M. at my house for our meeting time" will sound more attractive than "Well, I don't know when or where we would be meeting;but I hope you will consider joining us."

• Identify someone who is willing to go with you to visit the persons on your list. Make it your goal to become acquainted with each person you visit. Tell them about *Great Themes of the Bible*. Give them a copy of the study book for this group. Even if they choose not to attend the small group at this time, they will have an opportunity to read the book on their own. Tell each person the initial meeting time and location and how many weeks the group will meet. Invite them to become part of the group. Thank them for their time.

• Publicize the new *Great Themes of the Bible* study through as many channels as are available. Announce it during worship. Print notices in the church newsletter and bulletin and on the church Web site if you have one. Use free public event notices in community newspapers. Create flyers for mailing and posting in public places.

• A few days before the session begins, give a friendly phone call or send an e-mail to thank all persons you visited for their consideration and interest. Remind them of the time and location of the first meeting.

For more detailed instructions about starting and maintaining a small group, read *How to Start and Sustain a Faith-based Small Group*, by John D. Schroeder (Abingdon, 2003).

Leading a *Great Themes of the Bible* Small Group

A group may have one leader for all the sessions, or leadership may be rotated among the participants. Leaders do not need to be experts in Bible study because the role of the leader is to facilitate discussion rather than to impart information or teach a particular content. Leader and learner use the same book and share the same commitment to read and prepare for the *Great Themes of the Bible* session each week. So what does the leader actually do?

A Leader Prepares for the Session

Pray. Ask for God's guidance as you prepare to lead the session.

Read. Read the session and its Scriptures ahead of time. Jot down questions or insights that occur during the reading. Look at the leader/learner helps in the boxes.

Think about group participants. Who are they? What life issues or questions might they have about the theme? about the Scriptures?

Prepare the learning area. Gather any needed supplies, such as sheets of newsprint, markers, paper and pencils, Bibles, hymnals, audio-visual equipment, masking tape, a Bible dictionary, Bible commentaries, and a Bible atlas. If you are meeting in a classroom setting, arrange the chairs in a circle or around a table. Make sure that everyone will have a place to sit.

Prepare a worship center. Find a small table. Cover it with an attractive cloth. Place a candle in a candleholder on the center. Place matches nearby to light the candle. Place on the worship center a Bible or other items that relate to or illuminate the session focus on the worship center.

Pray. Before the participants arrive, pray for each one. Ask for God's blessing on your session. Offer thanks to God for the opportunity to lead the session.

A Leader Creates a Welcoming Atmosphere

Hospitality is a spiritual discipline. A leader helps create an environment that makes others feel welcome and that helps every participant experience the freedom to ask questions and to state opinions. Such an atmosphere is based upon mutual respect.

Greet participants as they arrive. Say their names. If the group is meeting for the first time, use nametags.

Listen. As group discussion unfolds, affirm the comments and ideas of participants. Avoid the temptation to dominate conversation or "correct" the ideas of other participants.

Affirm. Thank people for telling about what they think or feel. Acknowledge their contributions to discussion in positive ways, even if you disagree with their ideas.

A Leader Facilitates Discussion

Ask questions. Use the questions suggested in the leader/learner helps or other questions that occurred to you as you prepared for the session. Encourage others to ask questions.

Invite silent participants to contribute ideas. If someone in the group is quiet, you might say something such as, "I'm interested in what you are thinking." If they seem hesitant or shy, do not pressure them to speak. Do communicate your interest.

Gently redirect discussion when someone in the group dominates. You can do this in several ways. Remind the group as a whole that everyone's ideas are important. Invite them to respect one another and to allow others the opportunity to express their ideas. You can establish a group covenant that clarifies such respect for one another. Use structured methods such as going around the circle to allow everyone a chance to speak. Only as a last resort, speak to the person who dominates conversation after the group meeting.

Be willing to say, "I don't know." A leader is also a learner. You are not "teaching" a certain content to a group of "students." Instead, you are helping others and yourself to engage the great themes of the Bible as points of crossing to contemporary life and faith formation.

Introducing the Great Theme

COVENANT

GOD'S LIVING COVENANT

A tapestry hangs on my study wall. Threads of many colors and lengths are woven together to form a picture and tell a story. By themselves the threads are isolated; together they form a work of art. The Bible is like my tapestry. It is made up of a variety of themes, images, books, and stories written by different persons in different times and places. God, the master artist, has guided a people through the ages in weaving these diverse elements together into a work of great meaning and power. Brought together, all contribute to the message and value of the whole.

One major thread that runs through the entire Bible is the theme of *covenant*, a bond or an agreement that ties people together. In biblical times, a covenant usually was begun with a solemn oath accompanied by either a verbal formula or a symbolic action. Both parties were bound by this act to keep their promises and fulfill their obligations. Covenants were made between either equal or unequal parties and had legal and religious dimensions.

The Israelites thought of themselves as a people bound to Yahweh and to each other through "the blood of the covenant" (Exodus 24:8). Similarly, the early Christians saw in the Last Supper a formal rite that identified them as a covenant community, related to God through Christ's sacrifice.

This study will trace the covenant thread through the biblical tapestry, describing the major points at which the covenant between God and people was made, broken, renewed, or transformed. An earlier book in this series focused on covenant in the New Testament. (See *God's Project: Effective Christians*, by Kathie Hepler). This volume explores the covenant theme in the Old Testament.

We shall also consider covenants such as marriage and family, citizenship and community, our place in nature and the environment, and church membership as well as the less formal agreements we make when we begin a task, give our word, take out a loan, make a pledge, or develop a trusting relationship.

Viewing the covenant theme in the broad sweep of biblical understanding, we can identify a number of aspects of covenant that are relevant to our relationships and responsibilities as people of faith today.

- Our covenant relationship with God is a basic source of our **identity** as Christians. Through covenant, God formed a people bound to him in a relationship of redemptive grace and moral and religious obligation. Because God creates and saves us, we know we are God's; and we strive to live godly lives.

- God's covenant is with a people. As individuals, we belong to God because we are part of God's people. From the biblical perspective, covenant is primarily a **corporate** relationship; our personal relationship with God stems from that.

- God's covenant is for **service**. God formed a servant people. Being in covenant is a privilege, of course; but this is subordinate to our call to serve God, humanity, one another, and all creation.

- God's covenant is grounded in **love**. God covenants with us because God loves us and draws us into relationship. This is the difference between covenant and contract. A contract specifies benefits and obligations; a covenant is a loving relationship in which the give-and-take between partners becomes a free flow of love and gratitude.

- The biblical covenant is founded on **what one party has done for the other**. God delivered the people from bondage in Egypt and brought them to Sinai where they made a binding

16

commitment to be God's people forever. God sent Jesus to save all people from sin and death and into a life of covenant discipleship and eternal blessing.

- The covenant was begun with a **worship service** of inauguration, offering, and commitment. Covenant involves a vertical relationship of praise and adoration as well as horizontal responsibilities to care for all covenant members.

- The biblical covenant was **periodically renewed** in a formal service of covenant revitalization, which included a recitation of God's saving acts and a call to decision and recommitment. Our covenant identity is not automatically extended. It must be reaffirmed by each generation. Being human, we need regular reminders of who we are and what God requires of us.

- God **accepts people** as they are. There is no "means test" for God's covenant partners. When we do not measure up to God's expectations, repentance and forgiveness are always possible. A prodigal people are always welcome at the banquet table.

- God's covenant is **inclusive**. The covenant with Noah took in all creation. God is concerned for the well-being of all covenant members. Rich and poor, sick and able-bodied, weak and powerful, king and commoner, priest and petitioner, persons of all races, nations, and walks of life—all are recipients of God's creative gift. All are objects of God's restorative grace. All have a place in God's ultimate purpose for the fulfillment of the divine plan.

- From **God's side**, the covenant offers life, hope, mercy, and steadfast love. From **our side**, the covenant calls for gratitude expressed in worship, penitence, faithfulness, righteousness, and justice.

It is this understanding of biblical covenant that we explore in this study. We will examine several key Old Testament passages describing events and persons and their implications for covenant living in our time.

Session

1

TRUSTING GOD'S PROMISES

Genesis 9:1-17; 17; 2 Samuel 7

We all long for a sense of security and someone or something to trust. It is often difficult to trust promises that run counter to our experience and our logic. What can we trust as being sound and secure? God promised all creation never to send another flood, and the rainbow serves as a reminder that God is keeping this promise. God promised to give Abraham descendants and land, and these promises came true despite Abraham's doubts. God promised to secure David's lineage and throne, and Christians celebrate the eternal nature of this promise as fulfilled in Jesus Christ.

GATHERING

Greet one another. Share names, birthplaces, family and work situations, and a current challenge. Name the covenants to which we are committed and the benefits and obligations of each. Bow in prayer, giving thanks for the gifts of our covenants and asking for God's guidance and strength to fulfill them faithfully.

God's Covenants With Noah, Abraham, and David

Form three teams. Each team should choose a case study and its accompanying Scripture and commentary below. Team 1 will take "Trinity Church's Dilemma" and God's covenant with Noah (Genesis 9:1-17). Team 2 will take "Anton's Farm" and God's covenant with Abraham (Genesis 17). Team 3 will take "Connie's Position" and God's covenant with David (2 Samuel 7). Discuss the connections you see between Scripture and the case study in your group. How does God's covenant in Scripture inform the case study? Report your discussion to the entire group.

This session explores Old Testament covenants found in the stories of Noah, Abraham, and David. These exemplify the covenant aspects of universality, particularity, security, identity, and community. The biblical theme of covenant, based in the history of a specific people, throws light on the ways all people and communities are bound together and provides guidance for our relationships and decisions.

Trinity Church's Dilemma

Trinity Church has outgrown its space and needs a new building. Visitors like the congregation's friendliness, lively worship, and sense of mission but are turned off when they cannot find parking, have to squeeze into a pew, and see how cramped their children are in tiny classrooms. After an extensive search, the congregation located a forested hillside on the city's outskirts for a price they can afford. Developing it, however, will require cutting down trees and moving a significant amount of earth. Some members feel the loss of trees and potential runoff is too big a price to pay. Others think this site is ideal to meet their growth needs and argue that landscaping can include planting new trees. The covenant of congregational mission is in conflict with their covenant with the world of nature.

What are this congregation's options? What are the possible consequences of building on the hillside versus staying in their present location?

God's Covenant Is Universal (Genesis 9:1-17)

In the story of Noah, we meet the Hebrew belief in God as creator, judge, and covenant-maker. God created the world and human beings (Genesis 1–2); but viewing the extent of human wickedness, God said, "I am sorry that I have made them" and determined to "blot out from the earth the human beings I have created" (6:7). Though "the earth was corrupt" (6:11), God saw in Noah "a righteous man ... [for] Noah walked with God" (6:9). God would spare Noah and his family, saying, "I will establish my covenant with you; and you shall come into the ark" (6:18).

> The biblical covenant is most often thought of in relation to human beings, the chosen people, or people of faith. In what ways are all people and the world of nature included in God's covenant? What expectations does God place on covenant partners in the faith community that are different from those laid on all people? What are our covenant obligations to all people and creatures?

The rains descended, the floods came, and all life was destroyed except for Noah, his family, and the living things he sheltered in the ark (Chapter 7). Then the rain stopped, the waters receded, the dove returned, and the ark's occupants stepped on dry land, receiving God's command to "be fruitful and multiply" (8:17). Noah built an altar and made an offering. God promised to "never again curse the ground because of humankind" (verse 21) and to maintain the order of nature "as long as the earth endures" (verse 22).

The covenant with Noah has four features that can inform our contemporary lives just as they informed the lives that we read about in Scripture.

- *The covenant was introduced by God.* At divine initiative, God pledged to Noah and his descendants never again to destroy the earth and humankind (9:11). The promise of salvation rested in God's gracious act. Nothing that Noah, or any created being, could do would insure the continuation of life. With this covenant, creation was bound to God.

> *What responsibilities does God's covenant with creation place on the human partners to that covenant (described in Noah's story)? How does the story of God's covenant with Noah inform the situation at Trinity Church? How might the obligations of Trinity Church's covenant to grow and minister and the obligations of their covenant with God and nature be harmonized and honored? What would we do if faced with their dilemma?*

- *The covenant is unconditional.* God's grace and promise come with no strings attached. Just being God's creatures entitles us to God's blessing and protection. The birthright of all human beings through the covenant with Noah is God's acceptance and care. We can do nothing to deserve God's grace; it is a gift freely bestowed.

- *The covenant is universal and eternal.* It is an "everlasting covenant between God and every living creature" (9:16). God is concerned for the welfare of all creation. Nature is as much the object of God's caring and sustaining purpose as are human beings.

- *The sign of the covenant is the rainbow, a symbol of hope.* The rainbow that appears after a rainstorm brilliantly reminds us that the sun will indeed break through the clouds. The Genesis writer pointed to the rainbow as a sign of assurance. Just as surely as sunshine follows rain, so does the promise of God's goodness and mercy support human life.

Anton's Farm

Anton was a student of mine at Bethlehem Bible College. Now graduated, "Tony" serves as the youth minister at Christmas Lutheran Church in Bethlehem. He and his brothers own a farm south of town, which is surrounded by Israeli settlements. They have documents from Ottoman and British empires proving that this land has been in their family

> *What do you think of the clerk's response: "But we have papers from God"?*

for over a century. Yet, periodically, the settlers build new fences, roads, and houses that take in more of their farm. Their horse was shot, their dog stolen, and their land confiscated yard by yard. Each time Tony took me out to the farm, more of their land was gone. Finally, Tony's elder brother, Daoud, took their papers to the Israeli court. The clerk examined them carefully and then said, "Your papers are all in order, but we have papers from God." Years later, the case is still on appeal before the Israeli supreme court.

God's Covenant Is Particular (Genesis 17)

The story of the Hebrew people begins with Abraham and Sarah. God's covenant with their founding father and mother is the charter of their special relationship and mission. It is a covenant that helps us to understand the clerk's response in the case study of Anton's farm. The central importance of Abraham lies in the covenant relationship between Yahweh and his people that begins with him. This covenant had two parts: the gifts God promised to Abraham and his people and the response demanded of them.

What God Promised

- *A name and a blessing.* Yahweh adopted Abraham and his descendants as his people. Remembered as a person of faith and obedience, Abraham has become synonymous with faithfulness. In recognition of this, and to symbolize the divine promise to bless his progeny, God changed his name from *Abram* ("exalted ancestor") to *Abraham* ("ancestor of a multitude").
- *A son and a great people.* Abraham and Sarah were old and childless, yet God promised them Isaac as the first in a long line of descendants who would eventually become a nation (17:15-21). Abraham thought this was funny (verse 17); but "the LORD did for Sarah as he had promised. Sarah conceived and bore Abraham a son in his old age" (21:1b-2a). The people that came from Abraham and Sarah was great, not in the sense of being rich and powerful, but in being the fountainhead of two of the world's great peoples and faiths and in producing the Savior of the world.

- *To be his God.* Central to the covenant was the special relationship between Yahweh and Abraham: "I will establish my covenant between me and you ... to be God to you and to your offspring" (17:7). Although this relationship was to be extended through Isaac, God also bestowed a magnanimous blessing on Ishmael; and Abraham had him circumcised as well (verses 18-20, 23-27). The two sons and their descendants were bound to the same God in different ways.
- *A homeland.* The land of Canaan, to which Abraham had gone in obedience to God's call, was to be given to him and his descendants (verse 8). Their wanderings would come to an end, and they would settle down. Of course, due to their disobedience, they were to be uprooted from this land off and on; but they saw the covenant with Abraham as fixing Canaan as their base. Since this promise is given to all Abraham's descendants *before* the later distinction was made between Isaac and Ishmael, it could be seen to apply to the heirs of both— suggesting that Arabs and Jews might make a biblical case for belonging in that land today.

> *Does God's promise of land to Abraham trump the historical and legal claims of present occupants? What are the responsibilities of God's covenant partners toward those they consider to be outside the covenant?*
>
> *How do we resolve the tension between our concern for the rights of Abraham's blood descendants and those of brothers and sisters in Christ such as Tony and Daoud?*

- *A blessing to the nations.* These gifts were not for Israel's benefit alone. They were to be the means through which God would redeem humankind—a promise ultimately fulfilled in Jesus Christ. However, Israel was given the mission of showing to the world the gracious love, high ethical standards, and righteous judgment of God.

What God Requires

- *A spirit of faithfulness.* God called Abraham to leave the familiar for the unknown. This forced him to choose between remaining with his kindred and launching out in search of "the city which has foundations, whose architect and builder is God" (Hebrews 11:10). He was willing to risk, because he trusted God. He dared to leave comfort and forge a new path. As a pioneer, Abraham obeyed God's command, trusted God's guidance, and is thus viewed as a model of faith (Galatians 3:6-7).

> *How does God's call to a spirit of faithfulness contribute to our willingness to move forward in various life situations?*

- *A pilgrim identity.* Abraham moved from place to place, meeting Yahweh as he went. He set up altars at Shechem and Bethel to commemorate the events in which he received assurance of God's leading. Abraham kept moving toward the destination God held out for him, living in the hope that he would one day reach it. The external circumstances of life, and the way stations on the journey, were not as important to him as was the covenant bond that sustained and guided him on the way.

> *How does our covenant bond with God sustain and guide you as a pilgrim on a faith journey?*

- *Incorporation of heirs.* God's covenant was made with Abraham and his descendants. Those who came after him had to be instructed in its promises and responsibilities. They had to own the covenant as theirs. The sign of this initiation into the covenant community was the rite of circumcision (Genesis 17:10-14, 23-27). A distinctive physical mark, administered with pain and permanence to all in Abraham's household—including Ishmael—would henceforth clearly identify God's covenant partners.

> *How do we help our heirs in faith identify themselves as God's covenant partners? How can the local church help those children, newcomers, and others who come to our church families claim the covenant with God as their own?*

The covenant God made with Abraham includes us. As people of faith, we inherit its gifts and its demands. God has determined "that in Christ Jesus the blessing of Abraham might come to the Gentiles, so

> *In light of Paul's assertion that the covenant with Abraham was based on faith not lineage—thereby throwing it open to all who believe in Christ as Savior—is the Old Testament covenant with the Jews still valid? If so, in what ways? If not, what becomes of special claims to chosenness and land? What form should the covenant of particularity now take? What is our relationship and responsibility to Christians such as pAnton and Daoud? to Israeli Jews? to the land of Jesus' birth? to the God of Jews and Gentiles?*

that we might receive the promise of the Spirit through faith" (Galatians 3:14). We are brought into the covenant community, not through circumcision, but by God's grace through faith in Christ, as signified in the sacrament of baptism.

Connie's Position

Connie grew up in a Christian home. Her parents were laboring people and sacrificed to send her to college. She did well, earned an MBA, and started work as a buyer for a company doing business with suppliers in the developing world.

Connie is a church member but does not attend church regularly. She is drawing a good salary with benefits, and opportunities for advancement look good; yet Connie is gradually becoming aware that the low prices she is paying for clothing come at the cost of poor wages and working conditions in the

> *To what factors does Connie owe her position (house, name, community) in the corporate world? Who and what is responsible for the vast gap between her standard of living and that of the* maquiladora *workers? How might Connie better live into her covenant with God and God's children?*

maquiladoras ("factories") she does business with south of the border. Connie has worked hard to gain this position and feels she has rightfully earned her comfortable lifestyle, but her Christian upbringing gnaws at her conscience when she thinks of the long hours the *maquila* laborers put in and the hovels they must return to each night. The house she occupies, the name she has made for herself, and the select community she identifies with are in sharp tension with her covenant with the human family who are all equally children of God.

26

God's Covenant Offers Security, Identity, and Community (2 Samuel 7)

The covenant spotlight now falls on David. In this covenant, we learn that God is our source of power; and God is the One who offers true security, identity, and community. The story generates the following questions:

- *Who needs a house?* The scene opens with David sitting comfortably in his house of cedar. However, he felt guilty because, while he lived in splendor, the ark of Yahweh still resided in a tent. David wanted to build God a house, but Yahweh told Nathan the prophet that God did not need a dwelling place. All those years God had journeyed with the people. The God who had helped them secure their homeland was too great to be confined to a particular place. Instead, he offered to provide a house for David and his people. Finite human beings may need the security of a place to call home but not the Almighty One. In addition to a homeland, God through Nathan also promised to give David a house— a kingdom and a dynasty that would live after David through his offspring. The human need for continuity is to be met by the assurance that what David had achieved would persist in those who inherit his name and station.
- *What's in a name?* David had gained a great reputation. From a lowly shepherd boy, he rose to be anointed king (2 Samuel 5:2-4). David defeated the Philistines and brought peace to the land (5:17-25). He came home a conquering hero, danced before the ark (6:14-15), made offerings, blessed the people, and shared in a thanksgiving feast. He reached the pinnacle of success. Just at this point, however, God told Nathan to remind David of the source of his greatness (7:8-9). All his achievements had been brought about through the power of God. David's reputation meant nothing. His success was not achieved by his own strength. There was more in his name than meets the eye. David would need the eyes of faith to perceive the goodness and blessing that was to come through his name.

Roleplay a conversation among David, Connie, and God, with an interlocutor raising the five questions posed here, with "house" symbolizing security and continuity, "name" representing reputation, "who am I" focusing on identity, "who art Thou" directing attention to God, and "people" meaning community. Discuss: How do each of these factors influence Connie's career goals, job performance, lifestyle, and practice of her faith? How can David and God help Connie hold all these in proper balance? How might she live out her covenant with God and the human family in relation to the maquila *workers who produce the clothing she buys and sells?*

- *Who am I?* "Who am I, O Lord GOD?" David asked, "and what is my house, that you have brought me thus far"? (verse 18). In the next breath, David answered his own question. In himself he was nothing; but "because of your promise, and according to your own heart, you have wrought all this greatness, so that your servant may know it" (verse 21). David could have based his identity in his own achievements; but he was clear that his roots were in the promise and steadfast love of God, not in his own power, wealth, and position. He understood himself not as king but as God's servant. The covenant with David and his offspring was one where God was parent and they his children (verses 14-15). David's identity was as a child loved and disciplined by his heavenly Father.

- *Who art Thou?* David could be sure of who he was because he could trust the God who had chosen him and made possible his successes. David knew who he was because he knew who God was—great (verse 22) and faithful (verse 28). The covenant was sure because God could be trusted. Yahweh had brought the people out of slavery, through the desert, and into a land flowing with milk and honey. God's power had enabled David to secure a homeland and establish a house (dynasty, bloodline) through which God would eventually bring about the salvation of the world.

- *What forms a people?* From a human standpoint, a scraggly band of slaves had broken out of bondage, been toughened up in the desert, surprised some well-to-do farmers, and occupied a fertile territory. David had combined military skill and strategy with crack troops and considerable luck to set himself up as a rising young star among the kings of the Near East. Now he was on top of the heap, and his was a nation to be reckoned with. David did not see things from this human standpoint. His people had not pulled themselves up by their own bootstraps. No, they were God's people (verse 24), recipients of God's grace and deliverance. This awareness that they were formed in covenant with God made them a community. Their origin was in God's deliverance, their history the story of God's mighty acts, their future grounded in God's promise. Their mission was to be a blessing to all nations by proclaiming their God as Lord of the universe, so, in response to David's hymn, "Blessed be the LORD, the God of Israel, / from everlasting to everlasting. / All the people said 'Amen!' and praised the LORD" (1 Chronicles 16:35-36).

God's Covenant in Our Lives

Each of the Old Testament stories of God's covenant offers hope in the dimensions we explored. The covenant with Noah explores God's relationship with all humanity and nature. The covenant with Abraham illuminates the tensions between specialness and justice. The covenant with David emphasizes reliance on God rather than pride in achievement and the responsibility to use our position to serve the well-being of all in the human community. Think about issues in your personal lives, church, and society comparable to those faced by Trinity Church, Anton and Daoud, and Connie. Taken together, God's covenants with Noah, Abraham, and David have much to offer in the assurance of God's presence and power and in our ability to respond to God's guidance in the covenant relationship.

CLOSING WORSHIP

Pray for God's guidance in each life situation that calls us to respond to God's covenant relationship with us. If it is helpful, you may wish to name your life situation aloud. Close by singing "God, Who Stretched the Spangled Heavens."

Session

2

HONORING AND SERVING GOD

Exodus 19:1-6; 24:3-8; Joshua 24

Healthy, successful relationships depend on mutual commitment and responsibility. Life is full of choices. What does it mean to bear mutual responsibility for one another? What choice matters most? God's promise in Exodus 19 called for commitment and respect on both sides. If the people would honor God through obedience, God would treasure the people and set them apart. Joshua told the people that the most important choice they could make was to serve God.

GATHERING

Greet one another. List on a large sheet of paper areas of life in which commitment and responsibility are important. Pray together the following prayer: God of all people, help us as we look closely at the commitments and responsibilities of our covenants with one another and in the covenant you continue to offer to us. In Christ we pray. Amen.

Covenant Church Seeks to Be Faithful

Covenant Church has been in slow decline for ten years. Their neighborhood has changed. Members have died or moved away. Young people who went off to college or to find jobs have not returned. The church seems unable to attract replacements. With rising fuel costs, pastor's pension and health insurance, denominational financial obligations, and building maintenance, their shrinking membership—many on fixed income— are facing a budget crunch. The members are starting to wonder whether they may have to close the church or merge with another church. Neither option appeals to them.

> *How can Covenant Church best keep faith with their covenant to be the church? What might provide guidance for the period of discernment and transition they are entering? What would we do in their situation?*

Covenant Church has been in this community for over a century. Pictures of previous pastors line the walls. Seven of their young people have gone into pastoral ministry. A host of bygone saints are buried in the adjacent graveyard. Every nook and cranny of their crumbling building harbors treasured memories. How can they let all this go? Yet they cannot maintain the building, pay their pastor, and meet expenses much longer.

The members feel a strong sense of covenant with God, each other, and those who have gone before. To close down or join with another congregation feels like a betrayal of who they have been and are still called to be.

Sinai: The Covenant Offered (Exodus 19:1-6)

The people of Israel had been free of bondage for three months. They had left the drudgery of brickmaking for a day-to-day journey under the hot desert sun. No longer driven and fed by heartless captors, they instead had to fend for themselves; and they were worried about their next meal and where they would end up. Some longed for the security and comforts they had left behind. Others were still excited to be free and challenged by new prospects. Their clothes were wearing out, their muscles were aching, and their spirits were starting to sag with the sameness of the scenery and the arduous daily routine.

In this dispirited state, they reached the wilderness of Sinai and pitched their tents before an awesome mountain. Their leader, Moses, whose charismatic confrontation of the mighty Pharaoh had won their freedom, left them in camp to climb the volcanic mountain. There he met Yahweh, God of their liberation, and received a message for the bedraggled band encamped below.

Imagine that you are one of the Israelites trudging through the desert, remembering life in Egypt, nursing blistered feet, grumbling at Moses for ignoring your needs, and wondering what will happen next. How do you feel as you pitch camp tonight? What do you say to Moses as he leaves you behind to ascend the mountain?

The message Moses brought down to the people offered them a covenant that could transform a collection of weary, disheartened ex-slaves into a people with a purpose. The proof that Yahweh could deliver could be seen in what he had done for them already. He had sprung them from the clutches of their Egyptian slavemasters, led them through menacing waters, sustained them "on eagles' wings" through the uncharted wilderness, and had "brought you to myself" at this holy mountain. However, much more was offered. The people could become God's "treasured possession," a "priestly kingdom and a holy nation." Yahweh wanted to lay a special claim on them, give

Imagine that you are listening to Moses after he has come down the mountain. How would you respond to the offer he brings back from Yahweh? What does it mean to you to be called a "treasured possession," a "priestly kingdom," a "holy nation?" What kind of new expectations will this proposed covenant lay on you? Will you be up to it? Will it be worth it?

them a singular role, set them apart for unique responsibilities, and consecrate them for service to him alone (Deuteronomy 7:6; 14:2; 26:18; Isaiah 61:6; 1 Peter 2:5, 9). This was not just any run-of-the-mill

33

tribal deity making this offer; this was the God who reigns over the whole earth! (Exodus 9:29b; Psalm 24:1).

There was a catch, however. The people had covenant obligations, too. They had to "obey my voice and keep my covenant" (Exodus 19:5). What this would involve was spelled out later in the Ten Commandments, much of Deuteronomy, and the Book of Leviticus— a tall order, indeed!

Sinai: The Covenant Confirmed (Exodus 24:3-8)

Exodus 24 records a worship service during which the covenant at Sinai was constituted. The historic inauguration rite had two parts: a sacrifice offered at the foot of the mount of God and a ritual ascent by Moses, Aaron, and the elders.

> Discuss: What are the similarities and differences between this ancient ritual of covenant inauguration and our service of Holy Communion? How do we link Communion to our covenant with God in our own thinking and practice? What does God offer us in this covenant of Communion, and what are our covenant obligations?

Two types of sacrifice were carried out. One was the offering of an animal to be consumed by fire—a gift presented to God that could not be taken back. The other was a peace offering; a portion of the animal was eaten to symbolize the union between worshipers and God. Thus, the giving of self wholly to Yahweh and the communion of the people with the living God were ritualized.

Another essential element was the word of God spoken through the priests and the prophets. Following this, an altar was constructed surrounded by 12 stones representing the 12 tribes. Next came the blood ritual, which sealed the agreement. The altar symbolized the presence of Yahweh. The blood was sprinkled on the assembly only after they had heard the provisions of the covenant. This likely included the Ten Commandments and the Law code contained in Exodus 21:1–23:19.

The people's response to these covenant terms was, "All that the LORD has spoken we will do, and we will be obedient" (24:7b). This promise of allegiance now qualified them to receive the sprinkling of blood, which sealed their covenant relationship with Yahweh. This

34

order of participation in communion with God following proclamation of the Word is observed in the sacrament of the Lord's Supper today.

The second phase was the ascent of the mountain by Moses, Aaron and his two sons, and the heads of tribes and clans. At the summit, "they saw the God of Israel" (verse 10a). The covenant that had been ritualized below was now confirmed by divine revelation. Then, with Yahweh as host, they partook of a covenant meal (verse 11b), thus formalizing with food and drink a binding relationship with their God.

Thus, in this ancient covenant ritual, there were two stages. First, the word of interpretation was spoken, animals were sacrificed, God's presence was symbolized by blood cast on the altar, and—after taking a vow of obedience—the people were sprinkled with blood to secure the agreement. In the second act, leaders climbed the holy mount, Yahweh was encountered, and a sacramental meal was taken. The covenant had been enacted; a binding relationship had been established; and a people had been formed.[i]

The Martins' Family Covenant

Don and Erica Martin are doing well. Both have good jobs: Don as an elementary school principal and Erica as vice president of a growing real estate firm. They have a modest but comfortable home, nearly all paid for, in the historic district of a small city. They are active in church and community affairs. Their son, Bruce, is a high-school sports star likely to win an athletic scholarship when he goes to college next fall. Their daughter, Samantha, is an honor student and a budding violist in the middle-school orchestra. Their home is loaded with electronic sound and computer equipment. The walls of both kids' bedrooms are plastered with posters of pop and sports stars. Feeling cramped for space because of all their stuff, Don and Erica are now considering a move to a new development of million-dollar homes on the edge of town. This would mean buying a third car for the kids and new furniture to match the decor. Several of their friends have already made similar moves.

In the midst of their house search, the Martins discover that Erica is pregnant. This was not planned and is inconvenient to say the least. They have all the family they want, are embarked on promising careers, plan to move into a dream home, and are saving so both children can go to the college of their choice. The Martins' budget includes their church pledge and contributions to several local charities. Having another baby at this point in their lives would probably mean giving up their planned move, turning their communications room into a nursery, the kids' giving up getting their own car, and Erica cutting back on her real estate business—with a corresponding drop in income.

Read "The Martins' Family Covenant." Reflect silently for a few moments about what you have read. Draw a symbolic response expressing the feelings the situation evokes. Find a partner. Show one another your drawings and how they represent your feelings and thoughts about the Martin family. What does their church membership mean to them? What covenants have they made in the past? How are they keeping them? What guidelines—in Scripture, church teaching, rational decision-making, and previous experience—can they draw on in this choice between a new home and a new baby?

One obvious option is abortion. Before her pregnancy starts to show, Erica could have an abortion; and Bruce and Samantha and the Martins' friends would be none the wiser. The family's comfortable life could go on as envisioned. They could continue to fulfill all their obligations to jobs, church, and community. However, they would have to live with the knowledge that they had ended the potential life of an unwanted baby. Would this child have a fair chance growing up in a busy household with already-established patterns and priorities? Was it yet a real person at this early stage? Would they forever resent its intrusion into their cozy existence, or would they discover a transforming joy in this new presence in their home and in the challenge of nurturing a new life into maturity?

Undivided Loyalty (Joshua 24:1-28)

Many biblical scholars believe that ancient Israel held a service of covenant renewal every seven years when the Israelites reaffirmed the covenant into which their ancestors had entered at Sinai. This was to be done during the Festival of Booths (Deuteronomy 31:10-13). One such account is found in Joshua 24. Another was observed during the reformation under King Josiah (2 Kings 23). A third took place in the time of Ezra, after the return from exile, and is recorded in Nehemiah 9.

Preaching took place on these occasions, an example of which we find in Joshua 24. Joshua's two-part sermon on the covenant theme was delivered during the gathering at Shechem, between Mounts Ebal and Gerizim, described in Chapter 8.

Roleplay a conversation among three listeners to the Joshua sermon: one who is a true believer in Yahweh and ardent in pledging total commitment, a farmer concerned that giving up the Canaanite fertility rites could adversely affect his crops, and a third who thinks that "both/and" would be better than "either/or." What connections do you make between the circumstances of this passage and the contemporary situation of the Martin family? in other choices we must make in contemporary life? How might Joshua's call to the people of Israel help Don and Erica Martin? How might it help in our difficult choices about commitments and responsibilities?

In the first half of Chapter 24, through verse 13, Joshua recited the saving acts of Yahweh, carried out through the lives of the patriarchs and Moses and in the struggle to become established in Canaan. Then, from verse 14 on, Joshua issued a call to decision and the people responded. The spokesman of God invited the congregation to fear Yahweh and to serve him alone. They could no longer continue to carry the worthless baggage inherited from their ancestors, who were worshiping other gods even back in Egypt. This polytheistic practice was continuing in Canaan and had to cease. Because their neighbors' pagan fertility rites were intimately connected with agriculture, when the Israelite newcomers saw how lush the crops were, they assumed the worship of local deities had something to do with it. However, Joshua forcefully reminded them that the covenant at Sinai required them to worship Yahweh alone.

So this ancient sermon concluded with the ringing words: "Choose this day whom you will serve, whether the gods your ancestors served in the region beyond the River or the gods of the Amorites in whose land you are living; but as for me and my household, we will serve the LORD" (verse 15).

To this clarion call to decision, the people responded with enthusiastic clarity: "Far be it from us that we should forsake the LORD to serve other gods" (verse 16). They then echoed Joshua's sermon by rehearsing all Yahweh had done for them. Because Yahweh had stood by them, they would likewise strive to serve him as their one and only God. They had worshiped Yahweh and the Canaanite gods—the former out of historical loyalty, the latter for pragmatic reasons related to getting along with their neighbors and insuring a productive harvest. Now they were moving to make an exclusive commitment to the God of their origins.

In the sermon talkback, Joshua tested what he suspected might be a too-glib response. Caught up in the sensation of the moment, the people may have been simply mouthing what they thought he wanted to hear. So he chided them: "You say you will serve Yahweh, but do you mean it? To serve him will be too difficult for you. He is a holy God, high and lifted up, not one so readily swayed as the Amorite deities. Also, Yahweh is jealous. He will insist that you give up these other religious practices you have adopted and follow him only. That won't be as easy as making a verbal promise in this moment of high emotion. If you go back on your word, there'll be consequences. Yahweh has been good to you so far; but if you revert to your pagan practices, don't expect forgiveness next time around. Instead there will be punishment, even annihilation. So, Israel, you'd better be sure about this. Be sure you mean what you say."

> *What are the Martins' gods? What do they worship? What contemporary gods do we serve? (for example, pleasure, profit, comfort, achievement, conspicuous consumption, athletes, entertainers, politicians, and preachers). How might Joshua's call to exclusive devotion affect our attitudes and behavior in relation to each of these?*

These words may have sobered them up a bit, making them aware that this was a life-or-death commitment they were making. However, they repeated their vow: "We will serve the LORD! (verse 21). Again Joshua warned them: "Listen to what you are saying, folks. In time to come, this pledge may come back to haunt you." They replied, "Yes, we understand. If we break this vow, we know we are asking for trouble. We will accept Yahweh's retribution for our unfaithfulness." "Okay," Joshua said. "I see you

> *How do we respond to sermons calling for renewed commitment?*

really mean it. Now go act on it. Go home and destroy your pagan idols and altars. Clean up your act, starting now." The people responded, "Yes. The LORD our God we will serve, and him we will obey" (verse 24).

Then, just to make sure, Joshua recorded what happened. At Shechem, he wrote all the rules and regulations that would make the people's verbal commitment real. Henceforth, it would all be there in "the book of the law of God" (verse 26) that by their oath they would forevermore be held accountable. As a visible reminder, Joshua set up a stone marker under an oak tree in their sacred worship space. Getting their attention once again, Joshua warned the people a final time: "See this stone," he said. "It

> *What solemn pledges have we made in our lives? What helps us honor them? What reminders do we have of these covenants? How do these help keep us faithful?*

has heard what we have said. Every time we see the stone, it will tell us we have promised to worship Yahweh only." Having put this seal on the agreement, Joshua sent the people back to their home districts (verse 28).

Reminders of Our Covenants

We are thousands of years removed from the ancient covenants in Exodus and Joshua, yet what they represent is as close and real in our world as our own breath. We are God's people. We choose who or what we will worship. We continue to enter into covenants. Consider what our wedding rings and marriage certificates represent. Look at legal covenants such as mortgage amortization schedules, loan agreements, and contracts. Think about such things as certificates of adoption or baptism. Like Joshua's stone, these point to covenants with commitments and responsibilities.

Covenant Choices Matter

We return to the focus for this session. In church, family, and life in general, healthy, successful relationships depend on mutual commitment and responsibility. God's covenant calls us to bear mutual responsibility for one another. The choice to serve and honor God defines and guides our commitments and our responsibilities to one another.

CLOSING WORSHIP

Reflect silently on the call to "choose this day whom you will serve" (Joshua 24:15).

Write on an index card a covenant prayer that names a commitment or a responsibility that you feel called to honor. Carry this prayer with you during the week as a means of reminding you of your covenant. Conclude by singing "O God Our Help in Ages Past."

---

[1] From *The New Interpreter's Bible*, Vol. 1 (Abingdon Press, 1994); pages 880-81.

[2] For more information about this ritual, see *The New Interpreter's Bible*, Vol. 1, pages 880-881.

Session

3

GOD PROVIDES LEADERS

Judges 2:11-12; 4

We all long to be delivered from desperate situations, even those of our own making. Strong leaders may get results when no one else can. Where can we look for help? What characterizes a strong leader? Whenever the Hebrew people cried to God, God raised up a judge to save them. Deborah modeled strong leadership by obeying God and supporting Barak with her presence.

GATHERING

Greet one another. Mention current persons and situations in the news that are in need of prayer. Pray together the following prayer: God of all people, your covenant with us calls for us to take responsibility for needs in the world. We demonstrate our love for you by serving our churches and our neighbors in need. Give us wisdom and guidance as we explore your covenant message in the Book of Judges and what it can teach us about leadership. In Christ we pray. Amen.

The Covenant of Church Membership

Pastor Jeremy is greatly loved by his congregation. When he came to a dying church six years ago, his vitality and vision began attracting young families almost immediately. Within a year, Sunday attendance had jumped to nearly 100. In three years, the cramped Sunday school space was bulging at the seams, a youth group had been formed, a choir was up and running, and parking was at a premium. After five years, the congregation had outgrown their building; and the decision was made to buy a site and build elsewhere in the community.

These decisions, however, did not sit well with everyone. Older members who had been faithful during the dry years began to feel pushed to the margins by the newcomers. Others wanted to stay small and intimate. Some did not like the new social action emphasis of Jeremy and the progressive new members he had brought in. A building committee was formed, a new church site was chosen, and an architect was hired.

Pastor Jeremy's stellar leadership faced another complication. One Sunday, at the close of the service, he announced that he and his wife were getting a divorce. A couple of years later, he sent out a letter saying he had begun dating an attractive divorcee in the church. Some felt this was crossing a clear boundary for pastoral behavior. Although the congregation continued to grow, and most members were in full support of their pastor on this and other issues, there was grumbling around the edges. A few members stopped

> *Roleplay a conversation in which Pam and Susan try to persuade Ted and Doris to remain in the church. Then roleplay another in which Ted and Doris meet with Pastor Jeremy to explain their decision. Keep the focus in both scenarios on covenant-based reasons for staying or leaving. After the roleplays, discuss the following questions: In what ways is church membership a covenant relationship with God? with the congregation? How binding is this covenant? What are legitimate reasons for abrogating it? In what ways, if any, are the covenant responsibilities of leaders different from those of members?*

coming, and a couple of key leaders noisily announced that they were leaving the church. Pledges and contributions took a slight dip.

Most members, like Pam and Susan, believed that the covenant they had made when they joined the church involved a commitment to hang in whether fair weather or foul. However, some, such as Ted and Doris, felt that the covenant they had entered into had been violated by unwise decisions and questionable behavior. To keep faith with their own values they must sever their connections and look elsewhere for a spiritual home. They could no longer follow leadership in which they had lost confidence.

The Time of the Judges

During the period of the judges, from Joshua to Samuel, we see a settled farming people living more or less in harmony with the native Canaanites. However, they were forced to leave their fields period-ically to fight off new enemies— invading tribes from the desert east of the Jordan (Midianites, Ammonites, and Moabites) who

How does the conquest of Canaan compare to the settling of the United States of America?

were seeking to occupy the same fertile lands that had drawn them to this region years before. Because of their previous existence as hardy nomads, they had developed fighting prowess and hence had become the acknowledged military leaders of the land.

As a result of Joshua's covenant ceremony at Shechem, the people were bound together in covenant as a loose confederation of tribes, numbering perhaps 40,000 (Judges 5:8), composed of former invaders and original inhabitants who had intermarried, amalgamated, and were scattered throughout Palestine. Though the 12 tribes were distinct and self-governing, they were united by their covenant with Yahweh and the laws and duties to which this committed them. They gathered at the Gilgal sanctuary ever so often and

What connections, if any, do you see between the threat of invaders in the time of the judges and the threat of terrorism in the contemporary world? What role does religious leadership play in each situation?

43

responded to calls to arms when invaders threatened their territory and tranquility.

The Book of Judges, while not a chronological history, presents a series of snapshots of life and events centered around key leaders in this three-century period. The overall quality of their life together is aptly described in the last verse: "In those days there was no king in Israel; all the people did what was right in their own eyes" (21:25). It was a period of independence and individualism bordering on anarchy. There was no central authority, no power of law enforcement, and no sense of national solidarity. Being dispersed through the land, and all busy with everyday routines, it was easy to ignore covenant loyalties and obligations.

While some of the Israelites occupied the ruins of the hill towns they had conquered under Joshua, most of their settlements on the plains were in territory still controlled by Canaanite strongholds. Indeed, the first chapter of Judges suggests that their colonies were separated from each other by a string of Canaanite fortresses that they were unable to vanquish "because they had chariots of iron" (1:19).

Judges as Key Leaders

The word *judge*, used to identify the leaders, in most cases did not refer to legal administrators who presided over courts of law or governors who held continuing authority for ruling the tribes. The judges in this case were military champions who rose up in times of crisis, when life and property where threatened, to galvanize resistance, recruit a pick-up army, and defeat the foe. Chosen because of their bravery, wisdom, and daring, their leadership was accepted for the duration of the threat, after which they resumed their former status as ordinary citizens. The judges were of two types: military heroes (Othniel, Ehud, Deborah, Gideon, Jephthah, and

> *How does the perception that the judges were "guided by the Spirit of Yahweh" connect to the contemporary situation involving Pastor Jeremy's leadership? How does this biblical model of leadership inform perceptions of Pastor Jeremy? Why do you think some people have questions about his leadership?*

Samson) and less well-known city or district rulers (Shamgar, Tola, Jair, Ibzan, Elon, and Abdon). All were respected because the people believed they were guided by the Spirit of Yahweh.[1]

Because of their isolation and independence, however, neither occasional strong leadership nor the memory of past covenant ceremonies maintained covenant discipline and fidelity. The generation of Joshua "was gathered to their ancestors, and another generation grew up after them, who did not know the LORD or the work that he had done for Israel. Then the Israelites did what was evil in the sight of the LORD and worshiped the Baals; and they abandoned the LORD, the God of their ancestors, who had brought them out of the land of Egypt; they followed other gods, from among the gods of the peoples who were all around them, and they provoked the Lord to anger" (2:10b-12).

That the Israelites adopted the customs of their Canaanite neighbors is understandable— "when in Rome do as the Romans do." In a polytheistic setting, one could easily worship Yahweh and the god Baal and the goddess Astarte. It might even be more cool to go with the Canaanite deities, since, after all, Yahweh was the God of their past nomadic period, while Baal and Astarte were more useful for an agricultural existence. What need did they have for a guide in the wilderness when they were already settled in a fruitful land? It was far better to make offerings and sacrifices to deities that promised fertility, productivity, sexual pleasure, many children, and long life.

> *What similarities, if any, do you see in the situation of the Israelites during the time of the judges and in contemporary culture? How does the tendency to "do as the Romans do" inform our own attitudes about covenants and leadership? How does the tendency inform the tensions in Pastor's Jeremy's congregation?*

Disobedience, Defeat, and Deliverance

For the people of Israel, in spite of their tendency to worship the Canaanite gods, there was that covenant thing nagging at them. Back at Sinai, and again at Shechem, their forebears had committed them to an everlasting relationship with Yahweh that had unshakable obligations. The Book of Judges repeatedly reminded them that their experience in Canaan was cyclical—disobedience, defeat, and deliverance. When they slighted Yahweh worship to participate in the Canaanite cult, they flourished for a while; but their apostasy angered Yahweh, and punishment was sure to follow in the form of conquest and domination by the Canaanite city-states or invading desert tribes. This would trigger repentance and return to Yahweh, who would in turn raise up a leader to gather an army, win back their independence, and expand their territory. The ensuing prosperity would last for a while, the judge would die or return to civilian life, self-indulgence and complacency would set in, the people would lapse into unfaithfulness, and the cycle would repeat itself in the next generation. This is the story of the Book of Judges.[2] "Because this people have transgressed my covenant that I commanded their ancestors, and have not obeyed my voice, I will no longer drive out before them any of the nations that Joshua left when he died" (2:20-21), Yahweh said. So, concluded the writer, "In order to test Israel, ... the LORD had left those nations, not driving them out at once,

> What is your view of the philosophy of history espoused in the Book of Judges? Do you believe that political and military misfortune follows an idolatrous lifestyle? Do you believe that God acts through historical events to reward faithfulness and punish disobedience? Why or why not? Why is it—in contrast to the Judges theology—that sometimes the righteous suffer while evil seems to prosper?

and had not handed them over to Joshua" (verses 22-23). Israel, the people of the covenant, had failed the test.

Women in Leadership

The Deborah story is told in prose in Chapter 4 and in poetry in Chapter 5. Deborah, a prophetess similar to Joan of Arc of a later era, commissioned Barak to organize 10,000 troops from the tribes of Naphtali and Zebulun to take on Sisera, the general of the Canaanite King Jabin. The battle took place at Mount Tabor, overlooking the Plain of Esdraelon (also known as "Jezreel" or "Megiddo"), the site of many biblical battles. The vanquished general fled for his life, only to meet a grisly fate at the hands of another woman, Jael, who lured him into her tent to rest before dispatching him with a tent peg while he slept.

The people in the north had endured 20 years of Canaanite oppression under King Jabin, ruler of the Hazor city-state, which was buttressed by iron chariots, a fortified city, and clear military superiority. Unlike other judges, Deborah did not rise up just to meet this crisis but was already ruling the tribes in the Ephraim hill country prior to this military campaign. *Sisera* is not a Semitic name and likely belonged to the Sea Peoples, a group from Crete who landed on the Mediterranean coast in the 13th century B.C. Their invasion of the plains of Canaan from the west had collided with that of the Israelite tribes from the hills east of the Jordan.

Deborah was identified as the "wife of Lappidoth" (4:4), a Hebrew phrase that could also mean "fiery woman" or "spirited woman." She agreed to accompany Barak on the campaign and prophesied that Yahweh would lead them to victory.

> *Read Judges 4. What is your impression of Deborah's leadership in this passage?*

The victory over Sisera would bring no credit to Barak, however, because the triumph would be accomplished by a woman. Barak was led to assume this meant Deborah, but actually it was Jael. She was the wife of Heber the Kenite, who belonged to a group of traveling smiths (perhaps similar to modern-day gypsies), who had left the main tribe in the south (1:16). Barak's troops charged down the mountain, overwhelmed Sisera's larger force, and annihilated all except General Sisera (4:16). The victory was attributed to Yahweh's intervention (4:15), and gave the tribes control of a large, lush agricultural plain— the "fruit basket" of modern-day Israel.

From the commander of 900 iron chariots, the weary Sisera was reduced to being a fugitive. Coming across an encampment of Kenites, with whom King Jabin had a peaceful alliance, he thought he had found a haven, so he accepted the offer of bedouin hospitality: milk in place of the requested water and an apparently gracious woman to stand guard while he rested. What Sisera did not appreciate, however, was the ethnic tie between Kenites and Israelites. Apparently, "blood was thicker than water" for the wily Jael, whose job it was, as a woman, to pitch and take down the family tent, picked up hammer and peg—

> *Why do you think women are featured in this story? What is your response to the violent deeds of Deborah and Jael? What positive dimensions of leadership, if any, do you see in Deborah? in Barak? in Jael?*

tools she was accustomed to using—and killed Sisera. When Barak came along in hot pursuit of his vanquished foe, Jael invited him in and showed him her handiwork. The blustery general did not know whether to be glad or sad. His enemy was dead; but as in the battle where Deborah got top billing, once again a woman had beat him to the punch.

The prose account concludes by ascribing the victory to God (4:23), thus paving the way for the song in Chapter 5, which was Deborah's paean of praise to Yahweh for granting a great triumph over a despotic ruler.

The Teachings of Jesus

> *How do you respond to the understanding that Yahweh's covenant with Israel commits him to support them in warfare and endorses the annihilation of their enemies? What are the images of God implicit in these contrasting references? What does our covenant with God really offer and require?*

The covenant leadership presented by the writers of the Book of Judges contrasts sharply with Jesus' teachings. Compare the conviction of the writer of Judges that God was fighting on Israel's side with the statements of Jesus: "Blessed are the peacemakers" (Matthew 5:9), and "Love your enemies and pray for those who persecute you, so that you may be children of your Father in heaven; for he makes his sun rise on the evil and on the good, and sends rain on the righteous and on the unrighteous" (Matthew 5:44-45). While the covenant with God is paramount, Jesus has no intention of promoting warrior leadership.

Archbishop Oscar Romero: A Modern Judge?

Oscar Romero was a humble priest who, because of his reputation for piety and integrity, rose in the late 1970s to become archbishop of

El Salvador. His years in the priesthood were characterized by devotion to sacramental and pastoral duties and non-involvement in politics. The 14 wealthy families who, together with the hierarchy and the military, owned vast tracts of land, controlled the economy, and ruled the country thought that as a religious and social conservative, Romero would be a safe bet to lead the church.

However, the common people, who had been suffering under oppression ever since the Spanish conquest, were becoming restive. When strikes and non-violent protests were ignored or repressed, they started a clandestine guerilla war. Because the Second Vatican Council had given the people the Bible and the Mass in their own language and because a new generation of priests and nuns helped them understand God's promise of justice and liberation in the here-and-now, the people came to see that the God of Moses and Jesus was with them in their struggle.

Then, one of these priests, Rutilio Grande, a seminary classmate of Romero, was ambushed and killed by the military. This violent act stung Romero to the quick. He abandoned his neutral stance and became an outspoken advocate for the poor and marginalized. In his weekly radio addresses to the nation, he called on political and military leaders to stop persecuting his people. He visited sites of massacres and assassinations, buried the dead, comforted the bereaved, marched in demonstrations, and advocated in the halls of power.

> *Compare the situation of the Salvadoran people with that of the Israelites during the Judges period. How is the covenant leadership of Archbishop Romero similar to that of the judges? How is it different? How does it reflect the teachings of Jesus?*

In a particularly audacious radio message, he spoke directly to the army and police: "Brothers, ... you kill your own brother peasants; and in the face of an order to kill that is given by a man, the law of God should prevail that says: 'Thou shalt not kill.' No soldier is obliged to obey an order counter to the law of God. It is time now that you recover your conscience and obey its dictates rather than the command of sin.... In the name of God, and in the name of this long-suffering people, whose laments rise to heaven every day more tumultuous: I beseech you, I beg you, I command you: Stop the repression!"[3]

Two days later, Archbishop Romero was dead—felled by an assassin's bullet while celebrating Mass in the chapel of Divine Providence Hospital where he lived in a simple apartment. Not long before he died, knowing the powers would soon get to him, Romero predicted that if he were killed, he would rise in the Salvadoran people.

This has happened. His memory remains vivid, his presence is felt keenly by his people, and his words continue to inspire and guide them in their ongoing struggle for justice and liberation. Among his many

> *In what ways does obedience to God's covenant call us to involvement in social, economic, and political issues? How can we be "God's microphone"?*

poignant sayings is this call to covenant faithfulness: "If they don't let us speak, if they kill all the priests and the bishop too, and you are left, a people without priests, each one of you must be God's microphone, ... a messenger, a prophet. The church will always exist as long as there is one baptized person ... [who holds] aloft the banner of the Lord's truth and of his divine justice"[4]

God Does Not Abandon the People

The Book of Judges raises several issues regarding covenant leadership. In this session, we have looked at the contrast between the prophetic, sacrificial covenant leadership of Archbishop Romero and the warlike leadership of the judges; the dubious inevitability of the cycle of disobedience, defeat, deliverance; the nature of Deborah's leadership; the tendency to accommodate to the norms of popular culture; the accountability of leaders and members to the covenant of church membership; the contrast between images of God in Judges and in the teachings of Jesus. In spite of the violent nature of leadership presented in Judges, at its heart is a return to the covenant relationship with God. God never abandons the people of Israel.

In a world that includes leaders such as Pastor Jeremy, disgruntled church members, courageous martyrs, and everyday Christians who are trying to be faithful the best way they know how, God remains. God never abandons us. God calls us into covenant relationship.

CLOSING WORSHIP

To close this session, pray together the following prayer: God of all Creation, we thank you for the call to covenant living demonstrated through the Judges, for the challenge of exploring questions of faith, and the promise that salvation comes by grace through faith and not by "getting it right." In Christ we pray. Amen. Close by singing "Blest Be the Tie That Binds."

[1] From *The Interpreter's Dictionary of the Bible*, Vol. 2 (Abingdon Press, 1976); page 1014.

[2] From *The New Oxford Annotated Bible*; pages 353-54.

[3] From *Romero: A Life*, by James R. Brockman (Orbis Books, 1982); pages 241-42.

[4] From *The Violence of Love: The Pastoral Wisdom of Archbishop Oscar Romero*, by James R. Brockman (Harper & Row, 1988); page 172.

Session

4

PRAYER MAKES A DIFFERENCE

1 Samuel 7:3-13; 1 Kings 3

Praying for others shows our concern for them and engages us with their plight. Most people want to understand the world around them and learn to make wise choices in it. What is the role of prayer? What is the source of our capacity to care for others? What is the source of true wisdom? Samuel prayed for the Israelites when they were threatened by the Philistines, and God saved them. Solomon gained his tremendous wisdom by asking God for it, and God granted his prayer.

GATHERING

Greet one another. Share prayer requests for friends, families, church concerns, and current events. Identify choices and decisions that members are currently facing. Join hands and pray for wisdom, guidance, and support. Be mindful of these concerns as the session progresses.

Looking to God

In a complex and often violent world, individuals, communities, and nations are constantly faced with choices. People of faith look to God for guidance in choices that are life-giving, merciful, and just; but sometimes the answers are not so easy. Our beliefs and the harsh realities of a violent world come face to face. Read the following case studies about Ben and Sarah as they struggle for God's wisdom and guidance. Identify the tensions that emerge as their faith and the realities of the world around them come face to face.

Ben Martin

Ben Martin has been a Marine for ten years. He has served his country faithfully, and he is a devoted Christian who grew up in the church. Ben enlisted in the Marines out of a sense of duty and a patriotic love for the nation founded on high ideals by patriots such as George Washington, Thomas Jefferson, and Thomas Paine. After basic training, he served in various assignments, including a three-year stint as a recruiter. Ben's unit was one of the first sent to Iraq, with instructions to secure and guard oil installations. As a sergeant, he was soon put in charge of a small detail manning a checkpoint. In this capacity, Ben is becoming increasingly disturbed by what he sees as unnecessary violence inflicted on civilians passing through his station. On one occasion, his men fired on a vehicle that failed to stop, killing three of the four occupants. The fourth occupant stumbled out, badly wounded, shouting, "Why did you kill my brother? He did nothing to you!"

What tensions do you see between Ben's faith and his patriotism? How can he honor his covenant with God through his Christian faith and his covenant with his country as a Marine?

Ben struggles with the knowledge that he can no longer in good conscience participate in this kind of harassment of innocent people—especially since his understanding of the Marine code of conduct prohibits attacks on non-combatants. "Oh God," he prays, "what am I going to do?"

Reverend Sarah Bender

In her first church out of seminary, Sarah Bender's first funeral will be for a Vietnam veteran and will be held in the church sanctuary. His family, and the local Legion post, requested that an honor guard in uniform accompany the flag-draped casket into the church and be seated in the front row. They would then lead the exit procession down the aisle after the service and to the gravesite in the cemetery. Sarah felt uneasy about this amalgamation of Christian worship with military patriotism; but, being young and inexperienced, she hesitantly agreed to the arrangements. Garbed in pulpit gown and clerical collar, she stood outside the front door when the hearse arrived and the uniformed honor guard lined up to escort the casket up the steps. In consternation, she noticed that they were

> *Which do you think is more important, honoring the needs of the family at a time of death or upholding the view that guns are inappropriate in a church sanctuary? Explain your point of view.*

carrying rifles and seemed intent on bringing them into the church. She felt that this was going too far because the sanctuary is a place of peace and prayer and should not be desecrated by such symbols of violence and destruction. Ascending the steps and coming ever nearer, the soldiers towered over Sarah as they approached the sanctuary entrance. She felt scared, intimidated, angry, and perplexed. The men, the uniforms, the flag—well, yes, she had agreed to them, albeit reluctantly. What should she have said? done? She breathed a quick prayer for wisdom and strength.

The books of Samuel and Kings continue the theme of Judges. The covenant made the people of Israel unique among the nations. God had bound them in covenant to carry out the divine purpose in the world. Through priests and prophets, God judged their failings and guided their way. When they neglected the covenant and acted like other nations, God disciplined them. During the time of the judges, the people had to learn that, amidst the temptations of Canaanite polytheism and moral decadence, they could only maintain their survival and identity through loyalty to Yahweh and obedience to covenant standards and duties.

In the period covered by the books of Samuel and Kings (roughly 1100–587 B.C.), the issue is not so much cultural and religious accommodation as the power politics of imperial domination and expansion. The story narrates the transition from tribal confederation to monarchy; the lesson to be learned was that covenant faithfulness was to be manifested "not by might, nor by power, but by my spirit, says the LORD of hosts" (Zechariah 4:6). Under Samuel, they struggled with the choice to become a kingdom. Under Saul, they developed the traits and passions of nationalism. Under David, they became an expansionist empire. Under Solomon, they achieved the wealth and affluence of a commercial power. Under his successors they learned that the dominance and renown of nationhood also had a downside—corruption, degeneracy, rivalry and jealousy within, and envy, subversion, and assault from without.[1]

In the end, they had to experience the results of six centuries of spiritual unfaithfulness, inner decay, and external incursion—the loss of their favored position, cherished homeland, and prosperous lifestyle. They were conquered first by Assyria and then by Babylon, their unity as a nation was demolished, and they were scattered among the nations and forced to learn another way of being a covenant people of God.

Similar to most of the Old Testament, the events described in First and Second Samuel and First and Second Kings are told with prophetic interpretation. However, here the scene has changed from the stark contrast between the Yahweh of Sinai and the Baalim and Ashtaroth of Canaan. Instead, the Canaanites—Semites, like the Hebrews, who simply settled in the land sooner—were not seen as enemies or even rivals. Through intermarriage, trade, and treaty, the two peoples had merged. The Israelites were militarily stronger; but the culture, customs, and religious rites of the Canaanites had infiltrated the Israelite consciousness and the religion of Yahweh and in many ways had become dominant. The God of the consolidated people was called Yahweh, but they saw his character as being very much like that of Baal—a word that simply meant "lord" or "master."

The anonymous prophetic historians who wrote these books wanted the purity of the Yahweh faith restored and were nervous about the effect on covenant faithfulness of Israel's transition to monarchy and empire. Thus, they wrote prophetically about the ups and downs of the monarchy, critical of rulers and people for failing to live up to the moral and religious expectations of Yahweh's covenant people. While on the one hand celebrating the achievements of their nation under the prudence of Samuel, the courage of Saul, the ambition of David, and the wisdom of Solomon, they were also keenly aware of the ambiguities plaguing the growing nation: the perils of prosperity, complacency, inequality, and arrogance.

How can the story of Israel's transition from a tribal confederacy to a monarchy inform our view of the contemporary world? What similarities do you see between the contemporary world and the people of Israel during the time of Samuel, Saul, David, and Solomon? What might be the message of these prophetic writers to our country today?

The land was secured, the borders were extended, a central seat of government was established in Jerusalem, a temple replaced a tabernacle as the site of worship, life became comfortable, and social classes developed. The covenant commands—to put fidelity to Yahweh first, to treat all with justice, to care for widow and orphan as well as slave and sojourner, to speak truth and to deal honestly—were pushed to the margins of community and consciousness by the flush of success and affluence. The seeds of decay, division, downfall, and diaspora were sown, took root, and ultimately brought about the dissolution of a once-mighty people of promise and prosperity. This is the message of the prophetic writers of Samuel and Kings.

A Prayer of Covenant Faithfulness (1 Samuel 7:3-13)

With worship of the Baalim and Astartes rife in the land, Samuel appeared on the scene as an outspoken prophet, calling the people to return to Yahweh, to put away foreign gods, and to "direct your heart to the LORD, and serve him only, and he will deliver you out of the hand of the Philistines" (verse 3). They took his advice, covenant faithfulness was restored, the Philistines were routed, and Samuel rose to become the last and most famous of Israel's judges.

In an act of great symbolic significance, Samuel named the place of victory *Ebenezer*, meaning "stone of help" (verse 12), the same name as that of the site of an earlier defeat by the Philistines (4:2,10). That reversal had begun a period of national despondency in which the ark was non-functional and Yahweh seemed distant. To restore the people's confidence, Samuel, the new judge, enacted a ceremony of covenant renewal reminiscent of those led by Moses at Sinai and Joshua at Shechem. The Canaanite idols were disposed of; a rite of water-pouring was carried out, symbolizing repentance and purification; the people confessed their guilt; a lamb was sacrificed to the consuming fire; and the people implored Samuel to pray that Yahweh would save them from their Philistine tormenters.

Central feature in this covenant ritual is Samuel's role in interceding for his people (7:5)—a decisive answer to Eli's plea, "Who can make intercession" (2:25)? His prayer to Yahweh was for deliverance from the Philistine threat. It was answered by the action of the men of Israel who "went out of Mizpah and pursued the Philistines, and struck them down" (7:11). This event occurred at a place called Mizpah, meaning "watchtower," probably the Mizpah of Benjamin, a town on Samuel's judging circuit (verses 16-17), which later became a fortified city on the border between Israel and Judah.

> *Read the covenant renewal ceremony in 1 Samuel 7:3-13. What were the various parts of the rite? How do you see the significance of each? What was the effect of Samuel's prayer on God? on the people? Is the prayer of a leader more important than that of ordinary people? Why or why not? What is the appropriate place of prayer in the lives and actions of leaders?*

A Prayer for Wisdom (1 Kings 3)

Chapters 3–11 of First Kings recount the reign of Solomon—divided into two sections, its positive (Chapters 3–10) and negative (Chapter 11) aspects. The first part describes Solomon's majesty and accomplishments; the latter is a diatribe about the idolatry he entered into under the influence of his foreign wives and the strife caused by enemies within and without. The passage explored in this session (Chapter 3) describes the basis of his greatness—God's gift of wisdom in a vision—and illustrates its application in a concrete judicial case.[2]

The chapter begins with a brief reference to Solomon's alliance with Egypt brought about through his marriage with Pharaoh's daughter. Elsewhere in First Kings, we learn that early in his reign the

Canaanite-Philistine city of Gezer (antecedent of today's Gaza), on the Israel-Egypt border, was conquered by Egypt. The pharaoh gave the city to his daughter as a dowry, so through this marriage, Solomon got the city back (9:16-17).

First Kings 3:2-4 praises Solomon's devotion to Yahweh and faithful observance of the laws promulgated by his father, David, but also acknowledges that he and his people worshiped at high places, Canaanite altars consisting of rocks and trees situated on hilltops. This is an example of the amalgamation of Yahweh- and Baal-worship mentioned earlier. Although Solomon' successors were criticized for allowing high-place worship to continue (14:23; 15:14; 22:43), the writer excuses it here on the grounds that the Temple had not yet been built.

Prior to Solomon's construction of the Temple (described in Chapters 6–7), the main cultic center in the vicinity of Jerusalem was at Gibeon, a town five and a half miles northwest of the capital (present-day el-Jib). Solomon went there and spent the night, seeking a message from Yahweh. This was in keeping with an ancient Near-Eastern custom called "incubation dreaming," in which sleeping in a shrine was thought to induce revelatory visions. What he prayed to receive from God was the gift of wisdom, a practical kind of discernment that would help him rule justly and successfully. The young king's selfless request—asking not for longevity, wealth, or victory, but for discretion and good judgment—so delighted Yahweh that he promised Solomon what he did not ask for: fame, fortune, and wide acclaim throughout a long, flourishing reign. There was an important condition, though, a condition that always pertains in covenant relationships. Solomon faithfully had to "walk in my ways, keeping my statutes and my commandments," (3:14) as had his father, David (verses 4-15).

> *Think of times—present or past—when you have embarked on a new stage of life or career. What were you leaving behind? What were you moving into? What were your expectations? anxieties? other feelings? What did you pray for? How do these situations and prayers compare with those of Solomon? For any group members currently going through such transitions, invite prayer requests, lay on hands, and ask God for guidance, strength, and wisdom for each of them.*

Share parenting experiences of having to judge between competing claims of children. What factors influenced these decisions? How did you pray? How did you feel afterwards? How did the children respond? How did your wisdom and love come through? How might the prayers of Samuel and Solomon help you?

Solomon awoke from this dream, which had been a life-shaping spiritual encounter. He returned to Jerusalem where he made offerings to Yahweh before the ark of the covenant to express gratitude and seal his special covenant with God. He then threw a banquet for his entire household to celebrate the event.

A Test of Wisdom

Not long after this, God's gift of wisdom was put to the test. Two prostitutes living in the same house came to Solomon claiming ownership of the same infant. Both had given birth at about the same time; but one child had died, and one woman alleged the other had switched babies during the night. The newly wise king called for a sword and threatened to cut the child in half. One woman agreed, while the real mother earnestly offered the baby to the other rather than see it killed. Thus, the truth was revealed, the infant spared and reunited with its mother, and Solomon's reputation as a wise and just ruler and a man of God was greatly enhanced as word spread (3:16-28).

Back to Ben and Sarah

Samuel prayed for the Israelite's deliverance from the Philistines. Solomon prayed for wisdom. In both cases, the Bible reports that the prayers were answered. Samuel's prayer and God's answer of deliverance from the Philistines inspired the people to chase and defeat their enemy. Solomon's prayer for wisdom was not only a prayer for himself but for the covenant people as well. Both prayers reaped benefits for the people of Israel. Ben must deal with inner conflict about his Christian values in a wartime situation. Sarah must choose between the call to care for others and her strong views about the inappropriateness of guns in a sanctuary. The question for both of them emerges from the desire to honor God's living covenant, just as Samuel and Solomon sought to do. In both cases, prayer has the potential to benefit the people around them as well as themselves.

Prayer Benefits Others

The dilemmas of Ben and Sarah illustrate issues related to two types of covenant: the covenant of citizen with nation as republic or empire, and the covenant with God in tension with cultural practice. Persons of faith will seek God's guidance in these matters through prayer. This session began with a focus statement reminding us of some of the benefits of prayer. We engage ourselves with the plights of others and show them our concern when we pray for them. Our prayer for the plight of others may help us discover ways to reach out in action and thus become a part of healing their plight. When this happens, we choose to become partners with God. As we pray for wisdom, we also hold the potential to affect those around us in ways that lead to mercy, compassion, and justice. Once again, we become partners with God when we seek God's wisdom. Samuel and Solomon prayed. Ben and Sarah prayed. We, too, can pray.

Form two teams. Ask Team 1 to read the case study about Ben. Invite Team 2 to read the case study about Sarah. Ask each team to discuss how the prayers of Samuel and Solomon might help Ben and Sarah. What could they learn from these biblical stories that would help them? Ask Team 1 to write a prayer for Ben and Team 2 write a prayer for Sarah. Share the prayers with the entire group. What benefits do you see from these prayers for Ben and Sarah? for the people around them?

How does this transition compare with that of Israel during the transition from tribal confederation to monarchy to empire as described in the books of Samuel and Kings? What might be the message of the prophet Samuel to America at this point in history?

Read "Reverend Sarah Bender." Discuss: Why does Sarah object to the presence of guns in the sanctuary? Why is she uneasy about even the flag, uniforms, and a military aspect in the funeral service? What is the position and practice of pastor and people in your church on these matters? What parallels do you see between this situation and the amalgamation of Canaanite and Israelite worship practices in the time of Solomon? How does the "one nation under God" phrase in the Pledge of Allegiance relate to God's covenant commandment at Sinai: "Thou shalt not kill?" How might the prophetic writers of Samuel and Kings advise Sarah in her dilemma? What might Sarah say in her prayer? What would you decide?

CLOSING WORSHIP

Sing the hymn "Prayer Is the Soul's Sincere Desire" or another favorite hymn about prayer. Offer spontaneous prayers for individuals, the church, the nation, and the world. Close the session by praying together the Lord's Prayer.

[1] From *The New Interpreter's Bible*, Vol. 2 (Abingdon Press, 1994); pages 949-68.
[2] From *The New Interpreter's Bible*, Vol. 3 (Abingdon Press, 1994); pages 3-13.

Session

DEPENDING ON GOD'S POWER

1 Kings 18:20-39

S ometimes we realize we need to depend on a power greater than ourselves. What power can we depend on? At a critical moment, Elijah depended on God's power; and he was not disappointed.

GATHERING

Greet one another. Name the covenants identified so far in this study: with God, creation, church, life partners, family members, nation, and civil society. Pray silently about ways you have or have not been faithful to these covenants in the last week. Then pray this prayer together: We praise you, loving God, for the covenants that bind us together with you, your people, and your world. Forgive us for the times we have broken these. Thank you for the times they have kept us faithful. Guide us in this hour as we explore other dimensions of our covenant with you. Through Christ we pray. Amen.

Troubling the Waters and God's Power

Reverend Elton Strand is liberal on social issues and theology. During his first year at Elmdale Church, he has focused on building relationships—calling in every home, visiting Sunday school classes and fellowship groups, and preaching on non-controversial topics. He has found that the congregation is more conservative than he is; but most seem friendly and accepting, open to new ideas but uncomfortable with disagreement.

At the start of his second year, Pastor Elton feels it is time to become a bit more prophetic. Testing the waters at first, he begins inserting brief comments on social issues such as race, war and peace, immigration, and economic inequality into sermons on broader religious topics. During pastoral calls, he inquires about people's opinions on such matters as raising the minimum wage, national health care, and the death penalty before sharing his own opinion in a quiet, amicable manner. He proposes that the mission committee look into the housing conditions in their county's migrant labor camps. To the education committee, he suggests holding an adult study on the issue of homosexuality. With the finance committee, he suggests raising the budget percentage that goes to serve others to a tithe, as a starter.

How do you respond to Pastor Elton's movement toward a more prophetic ministry? How would your church respond? What factions, if any, do you think might emerge at the church? What connections do you see between the issue of a more prophetic local church ministry and God's power? What covenants do you see in this case study?

People comment on this change in their pastor's approach in private conversations. Some express uneasiness that he may be troubling the waters too much, preferring that the church steer clear of controversy. Others welcome his candor and the opportunity this affords for expressing honest differences of opinion. Some seem open to learn about the issues Pastor Elton is surfacing; others have their minds made up. Some want a pastor who "sticks to religion"; others welcome their pastor's pointing up the relevance of biblical faith to the issues of the day. A hint of developing factions is emerging.

End of Life Choices

Chris Jarrett, 59, has ALS, Lou Gehrig's disease. He has been dealing with it for seven years and is slowly going down hill. His wife, Dawn, works full-time to help pay his medical expenses; at home, she spends every waking moment caring for him. She is approaching exhaustion. Chris and Dawn have used up their savings and have taken a second mortgage to pay the mounting medical bills. Chris is becoming paralyzed, has to take nourishment through a straw, and communicates only through a raspy whisper. He will soon be completely bedridden. If his physical mobility continues to decline at the present rate, Chris will be completely paralyzed by the end of the year. The couple's insurance for in-home care has only three more months to go. When it runs out they do not know what they will do.

Identify Chris and Dawn's options. How could each of the actions they might take be seen as depending on God? How could the words of Scripture guide the Jarretts's decisions? What might help the Jarretts come to a fuller dependence on God as they wrestle with decisions? Can the hastening of death be considered a choice faithful to God's covenant? How can the doctor and their pastor be most helpful to them? What help might their church and class provide? What covenants do you see in this case study?

With future prospects looking increasingly grim, Chris and Dawn have talked about the possibility of ending his life. Dawn is more than willing to continue caring for him until he dies a natural death, but Chris is becoming despondent. He no longer finds any joy or purpose in living, hates being a burden to her, and sees no hope of anything on the horizon except further deterioration and misery. They discuss their options with Chris's doctor, who objectively describes possible ways of withdrawing or providing medications but whose Hippocratic oath prevents her from prescribing any way of ending life.

Chris and Dawn try to seek God's guidance in prayer, but their depressed spirits make God seem distant and unavailable. They know that God has promised to be present with them in time of trouble and that they should be able to depend on God for guidance, comfort, and strength at such a time as this. Their next move is to share their dilemma with their pastor.

A Prophet Emerges

Prophets during the Kings period were servants of God who discerned the trends of the times, were alert to threats within and without, and carried out acts of compassion with the poor and lowly and confrontation with the high and mighty. The premier example is Elijah—a complex character of many facets and amazing exploits—being fed by ravens (17:4-6), providing food and oil to a humble widow and restoring her dead son to life (17:8-24), outmaneuvering Jezebel's Canaanite prophets (Chapter 18), naming successors for the kings of Israel and Aram (19:15-16), and denouncing Ahab for stealing Naboth's vineyard (Chapter 21).

What is your definition of a prophet? How does it compare with the one given here? Who are some of today's prophets? What are their characteristics? Do they discern trends? warn us of dangers? show mercy? challenge the powerful? What are current issues that need a prophetic voice or action? In what ways can we be prophets?

Elijah came to the fore at a time when the people were suffering from a severe famine. Jezebel, Ahab's Phoenician queen and the power behind the throne, had just had a large group of Yahweh's prophets executed as part of her campaign to replace Yahweh worship with the cult of Baal. Elijah came from the village of Tishbe in the mountainous region of Gilead, west of the Jordan River. In his area, the Bedouin-like herders still followed the Yahweh tradition unaffected by the temptations of Canaanite culture and its settled, wanton lifestyle. This may account for his zealous opposition to what he saw as an evil and idolatrous violation of the sacred covenant with the one, true God.

A wild, charismatic figure, Elijah dressed like John the Baptist: camel's hair cloak and long, disheveled hair and beard. He made dramatic entrances and exits that disturbed the uneasy peace imposed by the despotic rule of Ahab and Jezebel. Strong, self-disciplined, energetic, he could run like the wind or fast for 40 days. Mystery surrounded him to the end, for he did not die a normal death but ascended into the heavens in a chariot of fire (2 Kings 2:11-12).

A Prophet Speaks

The focal event of Elijah's meteoric ministry was the spectacular contest with the priests of Baal on Mount Carmel, overlooking the Mediterranean Sea. The story begins in the third year of a pervasive drought. Elijah made clear to Ahab that it was Yahweh who controlled the rainfall, implying that it was the king's rejection of the covenant with Yahweh that incurred God's displeasure and brought on the drought (1 Kings 17:1). This direct challenge to the powerful ruler provoked Ahab's wrath, causing Elijah to flee back into the desert, where, at the direction of Yahweh, he hid in a gully and was fed by the birds (verses 2-7). Next, he headed

> *What divisive movements or issues in our time might correspond to the contest between Yahweh worship and the Baal cult addressed by Elijah? What guidance do we receive from our covenant with God in addressing these issues?*

north to the Phoenician city of Zarephath (in present-day Lebanon), where he lodged with a widow and helped her survive the famine by miraculously multiplying her supply of oil and meal and revived her dying son (verses 8-24).

Summoned by Yahweh to go see Ahab, Elijah moved inland to Samaria, Israel's capital, to seek to announce to the king that Yahweh would end the drought. On the way, he met Obadiah, one of the king's courtiers, whom Ahab had sent out looking for water and grass to nour-ish the royal horses. Obadiah was a secret Yahweh devotee, who had saved a hundred of Yahweh's prophets from Jezebel's vendetta. At first, he was glad to see Elijah, whom he highly revered, but was plunged into consternation when the prophet bid him return to the king and announce that Elijah was coming. He feared that he would be put to death by an angry Ahab when the unpredictable prophet did not show up as promised. However, Elijah reassured the faithful Obadiah that he would appear at the royal court that very day; and, true to his word, he did (18:1-16).

The encounter between king and prophet begins with the exchange of hostile accusations. Ahab called Elijah "troubler of Israel" (verse 17). Elijah threw the charge right back by saying it was not he but Ahab and his father King Omri who had been the troublemakers. Israel's deepening misfortune was due to their violation of the covenant, by departing from Yahweh worship to follow the Phoenician Baals. Then the prophet threw down the challenge. He invited Ahab to bring the priests of Baal and Asherah from the royal court, where they were living on the queen's dole, up to the Carmel promontory, and to send out word for all to come and see who would produce rain to break the drought. Would it be the noble cadre of seers, dressed in their royal finery, or Elijah the desert wild man clad in a camel's hair coat (verses 17-19)?

A Prophet Acts

The stage was set. The crowd had assembled. Elijah addressed the people directly: How long will you go limping with two different opinions? Get off the fence. Make up your mind. Will it be Yahweh you follow or Baal? The people remained silent. Which is the real God? he demanded. I'll show you! Lay wood for a fire, but don't light it. Bring two bulls. Let the Baal priests prepare one; I'll take the other. Let them call on your god (Elijah was accusing them of being on Baal's side.) to send down fire, and I'll call on Yahweh. Whichever sends fire is the true God. Sounds like a deal, said the people, seemingly confident that it would be Baal (verses 20-24).

> *Form teams of two or three. Discuss: What do we have in common with the characters in the story? How do we differ from them? How do you respond to the outcome? What challenges you about the story? What does the story say about the power of God? How does God act in our time to make known the divine presence, purpose, and power? Share responses in the total group.*

Next, Elijah issued the prophets of Baal the same challenge, which they accepted, perhaps secretly fearing they may have been in for a huge loss of face. All morning they circled the altar shouting, "O Baal, answer us!" But there was no response. Elijah watched patiently; but at noon, he taunted them: Where is your god? Is he asleep or lost or off on a trip or still thinking it over? This goaded the Baal prophets to more fervent efforts to elicit a response but all to no avail. They had come up empty. The curtain had been pulled away—there was no one there. Baal could not deliver. He was a fraud (verses 21-29).

Elijah seized the moment. He called the crowd in close. The people watched as he restored the altar of Yahweh, fallen into disrepair because of the switch to Baal worship. Elijah rebuilt it with 12 stones representing the 12 tribes, the original covenant partners back at Sinai and Shechem (Session 2). He dug a trench around the altar, laid the fire, cut up the bull, and placed its flesh on the stacked wood. Next, he ordered everything soaked with water, filling the trench. The people took it all in, waiting in suspense. The tension built (verses 30-35).

The moment of truth had arrived. Elijah lifted his voice to the God of Abraham, Isaac, and Jacob. Show them, he cried. Let them see that you are God and I am your prophet. Act, so their hearts may turn back to you. Then lightning struck! The resulting fire was so hot that wood, flesh, stones, dust, and even the water were all consumed. Nothing was left but a smoking pile of ashes. God had acted right before their eyes! Flushed with his triumph and eager to drive the point home, Elijah had the false prophets rounded up, hauled off to a nearby gully, and slaughtered to the last man (verses 36-40).

> *What enabled Elijah to win the confrontation with Baal and bring the rain? Was it his triumph or God's? What made him so confident that the lightning would strike and the rain would come? How can we gain the strength to confront the enemies of God? What challenges are we called to take on? How can we learn to depend on God as Elijah did? How does this story inform each of the case studies at the beginning of the session?*

Elijah returned to confront Ahab, who was still sitting stunned before the smoking altar. He told him to go have a bite to eat and wait for the rain to start, even though there was no sign of it. Elijah left, knelt down, bowed his head in either prayer or exhaustion. Several times, he sent his servant over to watch for rain clouds to appear across the sea. Finally, on the seventh trip, he spied a tiny cloud on the horizon. Before long, the wind came up, the sky turned black, and the storm was upon them. Ahab mounted his chariot and rode down the mountain and off toward the Plain of Jezreel ahead of the rain. However, Elijah, empowered by Yahweh, ran like the wind and beat him there (verses 41-46).

God's Power in Our Lives

The story of Elijah continues in Chapters 19–21, but the point is clear. The people's idolatry had been exposed. The perverted leadership of Ahab and Jezebel had been undermined. The empty promises of the priests of Baal and Asherah had been unmasked. The power of Yahweh had been vindicated. The covenant with Yahweh had been re-established. It was Yahweh, not Baal, who was the true fertility God. Only Yahweh could bring the rain that nourished the crops that fed his people. Baal was powerless, even to save the lives of his most devoted servants. The people had to be convinced by this irrefutable sign that they had to return to Yahweh and take up their covenant responsibilities once again.

Each of the case studies at the beginning of the session offers opportunities to depend upon the power of God. A church that wishes to become more involved in prophetic ministries can depend upon God's power to guide them. Persons who are dealing with end-of-life issues can rely upon God to provide the strength and presence they need during a difficult time. Each of the case studies also illustrates opportunities to explore covenant responsibilities: the responsibilities of a church, of a pastor to the congregation, of the congregation and the pastor to God, the responsibilities of a marriage covenant, and a couple's covenant with God for the stewardship of life. While specific answers to their situations are not always clear, the power of God is always present as we seek God's ways and God's answers.

CLOSING WORSHIP

Review the themes raised in this session: prophetic ministry; dependence on God; idolatry; end-of-life choices; and covenant relationships with God, in marriage, and in the church. Following a period of silent prayer and reflection, engage in a litany in which members respond with a word or phrase to complete each of the following:

O God, we thank you for . . . (member responses).

O God, we are sorry for . . . (member responses).

O God, we ask you for . . . (member responses).

O God, we offer you our . . . (member responses).

Through Jesus Christ our Lord. Amen.

In closing, sing either "O Love That Wilt Not Let Me Go" or "See How Great a Flame Aspires" (a Charles Wesley hymn the final verse of which is based on one aspect of this Elijah story).

Session

6

SEEKING RENEWAL

2 Kings 22–23

Life provides us with many opportunities for second chances and other forms of renewal. What spurs us to seek renewal? Reading the book of the covenant drove Josiah to lead the people in a magnificent ceremony of covenant renewal.

GATHERING

Sit silently in a semicircle around a window looking out on your churchyard and streets. Think of the troubled souls and relationships in your congregation and the needs in the community and the world beyond those streets. Ponder the covenant that binds you in God with those people and situations. Pray together this prayer: Loving God, we thank you for your care for us and for all people. As we explore another story of covenant renewal, keep us mindful of the needs of all you include within your covenant of love and reconciliation. Bind us together with those in our congregation, community, and world who are in need of your redeeming grace. Make our church a place of healing for the hurting and hope for the despairing. Renew in us an openness to your leading, a devotion to your purpose, and a commitment to serving in the name of your Son Jesus Christ, through whom we pray. Amen.

A God of Second Chances

Many areas of East St. Louis, Illinois, contrast starkly to the towering arch, sparkling high-rises, and upscale suburbs across the river. Deteriorating housing, potholed streets, boarded-up storefronts, rundown infrastructure—all characterize a town that as recently as 1957 was named an All-American City. Fifty years ago, East St. Louis had a population of 80,000, jobs were plentiful, and development was booming. Then the railroads and the stockyards gradually shut down, businesses moved away, white and black middle-class families went elsewhere, and the population fell to 31,000. With the decline of the tax base, the city lost revenue, cut services, and let sewers and streets decay and garbage pile up. Those who could not afford to move fell prey to corrupt politicians and predatory lenders. Drugs, crime, prostitution, gangs, and despair took over.

> *How does East St. Louis compare with the inner city nearest you or with the rural poverty in your area? What are the root causes of poverty?*

Many churches left, too, disregarding the social covenant that calls on community members to care for one another through thick and thin. Only one church agency stayed—the Lessie Bates Davis Neighborhood House. Its programs, which serve over 4,500 people each year, include emergency food assistance, affordable housing, job training, peacemaking between gangs, and training in life and survival skills. They are also heavily involved in advocacy for children and families on such issues as domestic violence, improved health care and education, affordable housing, public safety, and welfare reform.[1]

Bill Creeb, director of Lessie Bates Davis for 25 years, has this to say about policies and attitudes that affect the people with whom he works: "When budgets get slashed, social services are often ... cut first.... What they cut are the prevention programs. It's like communities that cut their police forces while the state builds more prisons.... I don't think we really want to look at the causes of poverty. We'd rather believe people who are poor are lazy and don't want to get jobs. This mentality has grown in recent decades. We as Christians often don't want to take the time to look at the complexity of an issue like welfare. We think just telling people to get a job will fix everything. Yet so many people on welfare are from families that have had people on welfare for generations, and the skills and attitudes they need to survive on their own simply aren't there."[2] Betty Tidwell, a caseworker at the Neighborhood House, adds: "God is a God of second chances, and so we work at providing second chances to people. We encourage people to reconnect to their church homes because we believe a spiritual base is important when you're struggling for self-sufficiency, a base that helps you know you're given a second chance to make your life right."[3]

> *What are the benefits and limitations of government welfare programs? How do we feel about the "poor people are lazy" mentality mentioned by Bill Creeb? Why do people and churches leave declining areas? Is this justified? Why or why not?*

Covenant Renewal

After Solomon, Israel split into Northern (Samaria) and Southern (Judah) kingdoms in 922 B.C. Ahab, whom we met in Session 5, was the seventh of 19 kings of Samaria before it fell to Assyria in 722. Josiah, who reigned from 639-08 B.C. and is the subject of this session, was the 16th of the 20 kings of Judah before it was conquered by Babylon in 586 and its people taken into exile (which we will explore in Session 7). Most of the kings of both nations were condemned by the writer of Kings for their unfaithfulness to Yahweh. All were measured by the standard of David, the "ideal" monarch; and only Hezekiah and Josiah received 100 percent approval ratings. The issue that appears again and again is the issue of *syncretism,* that is, "the worship of other gods." Josiah sought to renew faithfulness to Yahweh, to the rituals of the Temple, and to God's covenant with the people.[4]

The spirit of this reform is found in Chapters 5–30 of the Book of Deuteronomy, which emphasizes the inclusive nature of God's covenant with *all* God's people—rich and powerful as well as poor and marginalized; women, men, and children; kings and commoners; priests, prophets, and wise ones as well as those who are lame, halt, and blind. Even immigrants and sojourners are allowed to participate in some of the covenant rites and ceremonies. As the

> *Form four teams. Ask each team to read one of the following passages from Deuteronomy: 8:11-20; 10:17-20; 24:10-22; 30:15-20; summarize its central message in one sentence. Discuss: How would our lives change if we were to live by this dimension of covenant today? What is our covenant responsibility toward the persons and groups affected by systems and practices that ignore, exclude, or discriminate against certain persons and groups; unfair laws and policies that affect the poor adversely, such as low wages, poor working and living conditions, an inequitable criminal justice system, and polluted air, water, and soil; and moral choices and decisions that disregard or reject God's ways?*

Deuteronomist saw it, the people of Israel knew how the foreigners and outcasts felt, for long ago in Egypt they had been in such a position themselves. The king had no special privileges under the Deuteronomic covenant. In fact, he was the most accountable of all to its demands. He had to have his own private copy of the covenant scroll, and "he shall read in it all the days of his life, so that he may learn to fear the LORD his God, diligently observing all the words of this law and these statutes, neither exalting himself above other members of the community nor turning aside from the commandment" (Deuteronomy 17:19-20).

A Faithful King Takes Action

Josiah (which means in Hebrew "Yahweh gives, cures, or brings forth") came to the throne at the age of eight after the assassination of his father, King Amon. The power and reach of the Assyrian empire were declining, thus giving Josiah more latitude to institute a wide-reaching religious reform that involved removing all Assyrian idols and influence from places of worship. Under his father and grandfather, Amon and Manasseh (2 Kings 21:1-26), the level of immorality and idolatry had sunk to an all-time low. The author of Kings castigated them as being even worse than the pagan Assyrians whom they sought to serve and emulate. They increased the number of shrines to the Baalim and Asherah, ritual sacrifices and lewd rites led by depraved priests were encouraged, magicians and seers practiced necromancy and astrology, and human sacrifice reappeared (23:1-25). It is easy to see why the prophets Amos, Hosea, and Isaiah had spoken out so forcefully against the perversion into which Yahweh worship had fallen, degrading Yahweh to little more than an Assyrian Baal and his sanctuaries to mere "religious" brothels. Superstition, magic, degeneracy, and corruption had displaced the exalted adoration of the sovereign God. Truly, it was time for a change!

The reform, which began in 621 B.C., the 18th year of Josiah's reign, and paralleled that of Hezekiah almost a century earlier, involved the ruthless, uncompromising elimination of foreign shrines, rites, and priests from Judah and Assyrian-dominated Samaria (verse 15). The incident that sparked the reform was Josiah's initiation of a major Temple repair project during which "the book of the law" (actually a scroll) was found in a collection box

> *Read 2 Kings 22 and 23. Create a group mural highlighting the repair of the Temple, reading the book of the Law, consulting the prophetess Huldah, and celebrating the Passover. Which part of the story of Josiah's covenant renewal stands out most to you? Why?*

or pile of rubbish. Most scholars believe this was the main part of our present Book of Deuteronomy, which had likely been written or compiled secretly by the prophets from the north during the reign of Manasseh. It may well have been planted there by the good priest Hilkiah in hopes that, once presented to the devoted king, it would trigger a much-needed reform movement. After hearing the book of the Law, Josiah tore his clothes in repentance and then sent Hilkiah and others to seek God's guidance. They consulted the prophetess Huldah, who gave them a dire warning about the future of Judah and told them that the Lord had acknowledged Josiah's repentance and that he would be spared from seeing the disaster that would come to Judah because they had strayed from God's covenant. Josiah began a reform movement, thereby making possible the centralization of Yahweh worship in the Jerusalem Temple. The reform was highlighted by Josiah's triumphant celebration of a unique Passover in which he reaffirmed the Yahweh covenant and called all his people back to its faithful observance (verses 21-23).

On the political front, Josiah significantly expanded the kingdom of Judah in an apparent attempt to extend its borders to those reached under David. Areas recovered from the control of a weakened Assyria included Samaria (2 Kings 23:19), Galilee (2 Chronicles 34:6), and the Philistine coast of the Mediterranean, as indicated by the discovery of a Hebrew letter of this era at Yavneh Yam, a Judean coastal fort. Josiah was killed in 609 B.C. in a battle on the Plain of Megiddo in which he sided with the rising power of Babylon against the Egyptian Pharaoh Neco II in alliance with the remnants of the Assyrian Empire.[5] In three decades, he had brought his tiny nation from religious and moral decay to renewed dedication to the Yahweh covenant, and from weak vassalage in the Assyrian empire to being an expanded, independent force in Near Eastern politics. His leadership of a significant national resurgence earned the praise of Jeremiah (Jeremiah 22:15), who lived during his reign, as did the prophet Zephaniah (1:1; see also Jeremiah 1:2; 25:3; 36:21). The writer of Kings viewed him as the leading ruler in all of Judah's history (23:25).

A Covenant of Right Relations

I recently attended a church that had placed in the pews its current draft of a "Covenant of Right Relations," which reads in part as follows:

Preamble
To covenant with one another is to engage in the spiritual and everyday practice of loving more fully, longer, and better. Although this document expresses our written promise to each other, our true covenant lives and breathes in our actions. In times of growth we will use it to deepen our bonds with one another; during times when we are loving well, it will inspire us to love better; and in times of conflict, we will use it to guide us. We expect this covenant to be challenging, but we also expect it to inspire us to strengthen our relationships and deepen our sense of community.

Our Ideals and Our Living Practices
Welcoming and Hospitality. We practice hospitality, welcoming all those who enter. Greet people warmly; get acquainted with others; treat visitors as fellow worshipers; welcome newcomers into conversation; treat one another kindly outside of church as well as inside.

Furthering Diversity. We work to foster a multicultural and multi-generational community that sees diversity in all its manifestations as a sign of our strength. Engage with those who are different from us; challenge bigotry in all its forms; work to empower those who are disempowered; actively confront our assumptions through critical and studied examination of the forces that disadvantage some and privilege others.

Listening and Speaking. We listen with respect and attention and speak with care. Assume that people have good intentions; listen intentionally and compassionately; encourage people to speak without blaming or judging them when they do.

Serving Our Church Community. We serve our church community with generosity and good humor, and we will acknowledge the service of others. We honor all levels of service to the church, solicit the input of others, encourage people to make choices that balance their needs with the needs of others, invite others to join us in our activities, honor the right of others to say no.

Working With Conflict. We resolve conflicts directly, using openness and compassion. We make every effort to settle differences directly and openly, stay engaged with each other through difficult conversations, and hold ourselves responsible for hearing all sides.

Forgiveness and Reconciliation. We acknowledge our mistakes and shortcomings and are willing to forgive those of others. Acknowledge our own and others' imperfections; forgive ourselves and others; be accountable for keeping our promises; lovingly call each other to account for behavior that is hurtful to others.

Solidarity and Accompaniment. We support each other in times of joy and need. We help each other in times of crisis, recognize each other's talents, remind others of the spark of divinity within them, embrace our different cultural and faith traditions, and challenge each other to grow.

The document acknowledges that this is a covenant in process and invites further input, feedback, and improvement as well as expressing a commitment "to living and working with this draft covenant, adjusting the ideals, and expanding the examples to make it truly our own"[6]

I have no idea what congregational crisis, plan, or policy generated the development of this covenant; but it strikes me that a congregational covenant like this might be more faithful to the biblical tradition of covenant than the mission and vision statements—based on business and industry models—that are currently in vogue.

Josiah's reforms and the renewal of God's covenant can help us as we consider how our churches might be called to renewal. Parallels exist between a congregation's falling away from its original vision and commitment and the situation in Judah that prompted Josiah to act. If we are honest, we will see similar tendencies to neglect God's covenant in our own congregations. We should ask a few questions of ourselves. What guides policies, procedures, and relationships in our congregation? Would a covenant like this serve a useful purpose for us? What are the strengths and shortcomings of this one? What "ideals and living practices" might ours include? Josiah, with the help of Hilkiah, was able to recognize that they had fallen away and set about the task of a major religious reform and renewal of God's covenant.

CLOSING WORSHIP

Pray about ways you might renew God's covenant in your personal life and in your church.

---

[1] From "Nurturing Hope in a Landscape of Despair," by Paul Jeffrey, in *Response* (September, 2005); pages 32-38.

[2] From "Nurturing Hope"; pages 35-36.

[3] From "Nurturing Hope"; page 38.

[4] From *The New Interpreter's Study Bible* (Abingdon Press, 1994); pages 479-80.

[5] From *The New Oxford Annotated Bible* (Oxford University Press, 2001); page 572.

[6] From All Souls Church, Washington, D.C.; quoted with permission.

Session

SUFFERING CONSEQUENCES AND EXPERIENCING FORGIVENESS

2 Chronicles 36:15-23; Ezra 1:5-7; Psalm 137

Stubborn and prideful behavior often leads to painful consequences. What price is paid for such foolish choices? How do we
experience God's forgiveness? After Israel and Judah consistently
rebelled against God, the people went into exile. There they longed for
the relationship they had had with God. The people knew God had for-
given them when they were allowed to return home and rebuild.

GATHERING

Greet one another. Share past or recent misfortunes, personal or national, that
have led you to lose hope or to feel abandoned by God. How did you pray
during this time? How did you experience support and encouragement? How
can we be helpful to others at such times? Pray for God's help in finding
guidance and strength for understanding and dealing with tragedy in the
discussion of "exile" during this session.

81

9/11

September 11, 2001, was a day that will forever be etched in our memory. It was a time of national and personal disaster comparable to that experienced by the people of Jerusalem when their city was destroyed by the Babylonians in 587 B.C. They were taken into the insecurity of exile after that where they had only memories of a happy past, assurance of God's forgiving presence, and the prophets' promise of a brighter future to sustain them. We, likewise, have experienced an exile, a loss of blissful innocence, absence of security, restriction of freedoms, economic hardship, and enmeshment in a debilitating war. How are we dealing with our "exile" experience? Here is the response, written on September 14, 2001, of one couple, Phyllis and Orlando Rodriguez, who lost a son in the World Trade Center attack.

Not in Our Son's Name

Read "Not in Our Son's Name." Recall your feelings and response in the wake of 9/11. Discuss: What has been our nation's response? What feelings or thoughts do you have about the response? How would you pray in this situation? How might our nation heed the Rodriguezes' plea for a response that brings peace and justice?

"Our son Greg is among the many missing from the World Trade Center attack. Since we first heard the news, we have shared moments of grief, comfort, hope, despair, and fond memories with his wife, the two families, our friends and neighbors, his loving colleagues ..., and all the grieving families that meet daily....

"We see our hurt and anger reflected among everybody we meet. We cannot pay attention to the daily flow of news about the disasters. But we read enough of the news to sense that our government is heading in the direction of violent revenge, with the prospect of sons, daughters, parents, friends in distant lands dying, suffering, and nursing further grievances against us. It is not the way to go. It will not avenge our son's death. Not in our son's name.

"Our son died a victim of an inhuman ideology. Our actions should not serve the same purpose. Let us grieve. Let us reflect and pray. Let us think about a rational response that brings real peace and justice to our world. But let us not as a nation add to the inhumanity of our times."[1]

Just a Matter of Time

Fred Tryce lost the wife of his youth, Sarah, to breast cancer at the age of 41, leaving three small children for him to raise by himself. Life was lonely during those years. Once his children were in college, Fred met Janice Ziegler at the office. Janice was also a widow, ten years his junior, and had two teenagers at home. Fred and Janice fell in love and married. Twenty happy years passed. All five children got married, and Fred and Janice had 11 grandchildren between them.

Then Janice, barely 60, was diagnosed with breast cancer. "Oh no," moaned Fred, "not again! Not twice in one lifetime!" Janice had a mastectomy, underwent chemo and radiation, and appeared to be cured. After two years, however, the cancer reoccurred; and this time it had spread. Treatment was resumed, but gradually Janice grew weaker. Fred did everything possible to make her comfortable. The couple talked and prayed together and shared the best things of life as long as they could; but it grew increasingly apparent that is was now just a matter of time.

> *Read "Just a Matter of Time." What feelings or thoughts do you have about this situation? What gives Janice and Fred hope? What do you think they pray for? What would you pray for? What does their marriage covenant expect of them? Who do we know in similar circumstances? What does our covenant with them call for from us?*

Exile as Historical Reality

The term *exile*, as most commonly used in biblical studies, refers to the Babylonian conquest when most Judeans were forced to leave their homes and migrate to Babylonia. It began with the first deportation in 598 B.C. (Esther 2:6; Matthew 1:11), and continued with a second, more wholesale expulsion in 587 (described in 2 Chronicles 36:15-21). This was followed by a third banishment of a smaller number of leaders and artisans in 582, implemented by the Babylonians in retaliation for the assassination of their puppet governor Gedaliah (2 Kings 25:22-26; Jeremiah 52:30). At that time, many fled to Egypt where they were soon joined by the prophet Jeremiah (Jeremiah 40–44). The Exile lasted until 538, when the order was given by King Cyrus of Persia giving permission for some to return. Later, in 515, many more went back to help rebuild the Temple, as reported in Ezra 1:5-7. Thus, the Exile was a period of 40 to 85 years. The numbers involved vary from the total of only 4,600 reported in Jeremiah 52:30, to the 10,000 mentioned in 2 Kings 24:14 for just the first of the three deportations.

After reading the accounts of the Exile in Scripture and in this commentary, create a news report of the event. Have one member be an embedded reporter among the exiles, interviewing persons left behind in Judah, on the forced desert march, and after arrival in Babylon. Ask: What has happened to you, your family, your home, your neighbors, your temple, and your faith? How has this affected you? What caused it? How are you feeling? What will you do? Where is God in all this? What are you praying for? Then reflect together on how we might feel and react in the midst of such a calamity.

Not much is known about conditions in Judah during this period. Jeremiah 40 suggests that many were left behind, while 2 Kings 24:14 and 25:12 indicate that only the peasant class stayed to till the land. However, in 2 Chronicles 36:21, the land is described as lying "desolate," implying a place barren of all living things. Likewise, Jeremiah 44:2 indicates that the territory was empty.

Accounts of the situation of the exiles in Babylon are almost as sparse. Jeremiah 29:5-6 speaks of a relatively permanent settlement and considerable freedom of movement. Ezekiel 8:1 and 20:1 describe a group of community elders coming to consult with Ezekiel. Ezekiel 1:1 and Ezra 1:4 and 8:15-17 indicate that there were several settlements of Jews located in the land. Ezra 8:17 suggests the presence of temples. The remaining of many Jews in Babylon, even after some returned to Judah, is indicated by the continuing migration of smaller groups under Ezra and Nehemiah and the continuing influence of the Jewish community there on reform and renewal movements back in Palestine, even down to the New Testament era.

The Exile was a time when synagogues replaced the Jerusalem Temple as the principal places of worship; when teaching elders (rabbis) emerged alongside priests as the predominant religious leaders; when a viable Jewish faith and reliance on God developed apart from preoccupation with the land and the Temple; and when customs, traditions, interpretations of Scripture, and biblical scholars combined to shape a new identity for the Jewish people and a new face for their religious faith, which we now know as Judaism.

Exile as Biblical Truth

The long-term biblical significance of exile is much less historical than it is theological. The removal of the people of Judah from the comforts of their homeland and their forced march into unfamiliar, hostile territory is seen by many biblical writers as God's judgment on their sin and unfaithfulness to the covenant. Their return from exile to the land of promise is viewed as a mark of God's faithfulness to his side of the covenant relationship. The conditions for return and an end to exile—repentance and a change of heart and life—has become the standard requirement for all the wayward to be received back into God's good graces (Jeremiah 24 and 31; Ezekiel 18; Lamentations 5). The promise of return in Isaiah 40–48 has been a source of hope and a sign of God's benevolent grace to many despondent, suffering, alienated believers throughout the centuries.

The main biblical interpreters of the significance of the exile were the prophets Jeremiah, Ezekiel, Second Isaiah (Isaiah 40–55), Habakkuk, the author of Lamentations (traditionally thought to be Jeremiah), the poems in Deuteronomy 32; Psalm 137; and Isaiah 13-14, 21, and 63, and the priestly writers of Leviticus 17–26 and Ezekiel 40–48. Jeremiah, writing in Jerusalem, and Ezekiel and Second Isaiah, with the exiles in Babylon, agreed for the most part in seeing Judah's experience of conquest, expulsion, and forcible resettlement as Yahweh's punishment on a disobedient, idolatrous, and immoral people. If the

> *What connections do you see in the experience of exile and the experiences described in "9/11" and "A Matter of Time"? What might be the message of the prophets to us in our exile experiences? What might faithfulness to God's covenant require of us now?*

people would respond in faith with devout penitence and covenant renewal, however, God would be gracious to forgive, restore, and reestablish them in his divine favor (Isaiah 54:9-10; Jeremiah 31:2-3). A new covenant of heartfelt devotion (Jeremiah 31:31-34) would be born out of their experience of calamity and despair (Ezekiel 36:26) and bind them to God as God's servants and witnesses to all the world of his universal sovereignty (Isaiah 43:10).

Habakkuk (1:12–2:4) called the people of the early years of exile to a life of trust and faith in the covenant God, while another, writing in his name, scorned the already-declining Babylonian empire (Habakkuk 2:7-19). Lamentations and the Old Testament poems mentioned above express the people's anguish and despair and offer encouragement and hope of better days to come. The priestly writers called the people to purge themselves of all the sins and impurities that would have angered Yahweh and brought about exile catastrophe. The expe-

> *Discuss: Do you agree with the Chronicler's interpretation of the Exile as God's punishment for covenant unfaithfulness? Do you believe that God causes man-made or physical disasters as judgment on disobedience? How do we experience God's judgment? God's forgiving grace?*

rience of exile and the hope of restoration, as interpreted by these biblical writers, form the Old Testament precursor to the redemptive theology of suffering and resurrection embodied in the cross and resurrection of Jesus Christ.

Exile as a People's Experience

With this overview of the Exile and its significance, we turn now to a detailed examination of the passages selected for study in this session.

The four passages, in sequence, tell the 70-year Exile story. The first, 2 Chronicles 36:15-21, describes the people's unfaithfulness; God's patient, loving reminders; their blithe rejection of God's prophetic messengers; God's angry punishment through the agency of the Chaldean (Babylonian) army; the destruction of Jerusalem and its temple; their removal to Babylon; and the desolation of a once-fertile land laid waste—all in fulfillment of God's purposes. The second, Psalm 137, voices the exiles' forlorn lament at being separated from all they once held dear and then their determination to return to faithful observance of God's covenant. The third, 2 Chronicles 36:22-23, speaks of Cyrus of Persia's edict allowing the exiles to return to Jerusalem and rebuild the Temple—also a part of the divine plan. In the fourth, Ezra 1:5-7, people and precious goods are assembled for the return and rebuilding soon to take place.

> *Read 2 Chronicles 36:15-23; Ezra 1:5-7; and Psalm 137. What do you think the Exile calamity meant to the individuals involved. Recall disasters in recent history: the 9/11 attacks, the bombings of Iraq and Afghanistan, the Asian tsunami, hurricanes Katrina and Rita, and personal tragedies like that of Fred and Janice. How were individuals and families affected by these? Were they being punished? If so, for what? If not, why did these things happen? What constitutes a faithful response to catastrophe by the victims? by fellow human beings? by Christians?*

2 Chronicles 36:15-21: Consequences of Covenant-Breaking

Yahweh, the covenant God who had faithfully stood by their forebears from time immemorial, had been lovingly striving to bring his wayward people back to him. However, they spurned his messengers, the prophets, until God's patience had been exhausted. Their time was up. Bring on the Chaldeans! Let the judgment fall! Young and old, healthy and frail—all would fall to the invaders' sword. The treasury was sacked, the Temple burned, the city walls demolished, and palatial homes destroyed and looted. The survivors were taken in chains by forced march across the desert to Babylon where they became slaves to their conquerors. The land they left behind would lie fallow for 70 years (a symbolic number), experiencing an enforced "sabbath rest" and observing a covenant requirement that the people had been neglecting (Leviticus 25:1-7; 26:27-39). All this was as the prophet Jeremiah had predicted (Jeremiah 25;11-12).

Psalm 137: Covenant Faithfulness Restored

The poet depicted the dejected mood of the bedraggled exiles in graphic imagery. Weary from their harsh overland journey, they collapsed on the banks of the Tigris and Euphrates to moisten their cracked lips with fresh water. Looking up, they saw the turrets and towers of a strange city and immediately broke into sobs with memories of the demolished city they had left behind (verse 1). They brought with them the instruments to make music in praise of Yahweh; and their captors taunted them with requests to sing the happy songs of a shattered, unrecoverable past. However, they had no heart for singing in this God-forsaken situation, so silently they hung their lyres on the nearest tree (verses 2-3).

> Write responses to these questions: What is my "strange land"? How do I feel there? What do I need to do to be able to sing God's song there (for example, to be faithful)? What help do I need to sing it? Share these reflections in groups of three. Invite those who are willing to share theirs in the total group. Pray for each person in their struggle, asking for God's sustaining strength, a fresh vision of hope, and support for singing a song of covenant faithfulness.

With our precious Temple in ruins, mourning the loss of loved ones, having lost everything but the rags on our backs, footsore and haggard from a harrowing desert trek, how can we possibly sing? We are in no mood to worship! (verse 4). But wait! All may not be lost! We still have our memories. The Holy City—and the God we worshiped there—still live in our hearts and minds. We still know who we are. No one can force us to give that up. Our bodies may be weak from hunger and exertion; our mouths may be parched from thirst, but we remember! We are people of an everlasting covenant. We will be faithful! All other pleasures pale before this one constant truth: The God we knew in Jerusalem lives! That God is with us here. God is faithful to his promise. We will return to faithful living, too. We will observe the covenant once again! (verses 5-6).

As for the Babylonians, and their allies, the Edomites, who helped them destroy our beloved city, they will get their comeuppance soon enough. Their destiny is bleak indeed (verses 7-9). "All who take the sword will perish by the sword" (Matthew 26:52).

2 Chronicles 36:22-23: The Covenant God Fulfills a Promise

The long, painful years of exile were coming to an end. When Cyrus of Persia conquered the waning Babylonian empire, one of his first acts in response to Yahweh's prodding was to announce that the chastened exiles were free to go home, again fulfilling a prediction of Jeremiah (29:10-14).

The Chronicler had the pagan king include in his edict a humble acknowledgement that the power and success he had gained were due to Yahweh's providence. In gratitude, he would commission and fund the reconstruction of Yahweh's dwelling place, the Jerusalem Temple.

Ezra 1:5-7: A Covenant People on the March

God had been acting in the hearts of the Judean elders as well, and they were ready for the return journey and the building project. Those staying behind brought out of hiding the treasures their grandparents had carried with them from Jerusalem to help finance the trip and the new edifice, which would be costly. Cyrus raided his pagan shrines to contribute the Temple implements and ornaments, originally stolen by the Babylonians, which he had confiscated from them. All was ready for the exiles' joyous return to their beloved homeland to undertake the restoration of their cherished place of worship.

Our Hope and God's Call

Even in the midst of exile and despair, the Bible shows that the people of Israel never ceased to understand themselves as God's covenant people. God's grace and forgiveness offered hope in their despair and called them to renewal. As members of God's covenant community, we can find the same hope even through our misfortunes. We will also find that we are called to embody God's living covenant in our lives. God calls us to be a people who seek to find our sense of security, identity, and community in God's universal covenant; to honor and serve

God with undivided loyalty; to pray lovingly and wisely; to depend on God for strength to speak and act prophetically; to act in renewing ways in church and society; and to be faithful to God's covenant in the midst of trials and troubles.

CLOSING WORSHIP

Review the Scriptures and themes of the seven sessions in this study. Read the closing paragraph of this session, "Our Hope and God's Call." Pray silently about ways you might embody God's living covenant in your individual life and in the life of your congregation. Close by singing "Amazing Grace" or "Many Gifts, One Spirit."

[1] From *September 11th Families for Peaceful Tomorrows: Turning Our Grief Into Action for Peace*, by David Potorti, et al (RDV Books, 2003); pages 22-23.

Appendix

Background Scriptures for
"Covenant: God's Living Covenant"

Genesis 9:1-17	1 Samuel 7:3-13
Genesis 17	1 Kings 3
2 Samuel 7	1 Kings 18:20-39
Exodus 19:1-6	2 Kings 22–23
Exodus 24:3-8	2 Chronicles 36:15-21
Joshua 24	Psalm 137
Judges 2:11-12	2 Chronicles 36:22-23
Judges 4	Ezra 1:5-7

The Committee on the Uniform Series

The Committee on the Uniform Series (CUS) is made up of persons appointed by their respective denominations, which, although differing in certain elements of faith and polity, hold a common faith in Jesus Christ, the Son of God, as Lord and Savior, whose saving gospel is to be taught to all humankind. CUS has about 70 members who represent 19 Protestant denominations in the US and Canada, who work together to develop the International Bible Lessons for Christian Teaching. A team from this committee develops the cycles of Scriptures and themes that form the backbone of the Bible lesson development guides. The cycles present a balance between Old and New Testaments, although the weight is on the latter. Cycles through 2016 are organized around the following themes: creation, call, covenant, Christ, community, commitment, God, hope, worship, tradition, faith, and justice.

—MARVIN CROPSEY,
Chair, Committee on the Uniform Series